"Jennifer Banks's spectacular book *Natality* considers Hannah Arendt's idea that humans 'are not born in order to die but in order to begin.'" —Caitrin Keiper, *Plough*, Editors' Picks

"In her fascinating new book, *Natality*, Jennifer Banks . . . lets her own sense of maternal astonishment lead her where wonder has led thinkers for millennia, to philosophy. The wisdom she uncovers has much to do with birth, as the book's subtitle promises, and even more with what the irreducibly strange miracle of our entrance into the world tells us about the gift we have been given, not only of life but of free will." —Cassandra Nelson, *Comment*

"Banks offers a sweeping view of 'birth's full spectrum and diversity.' . . . *Natality* acts first to provoke and to suggest the open-endedness of our potential. . . . Banks shows us how others have exerted themselves in new ways, and allows us to imagine the possibility of such breakages and makings." —Ron Slate, *On the Seawall*

"[This] provocative debut explores what it might mean to center human experience in natality. . . . Banks highlights moments when her subjects' writings were in dialogue [and] builds those connections herself through unusual biographical juxtapositions, making for a layered, introspective study. This is an enlightening look at 'what it means to be born human.'" —*Publishers Weekly*

"Birth is humanity's greatest unexplored subject, Jennifer Banks writes in her excellent *Natality*. . . . [A]n investigation of birth itself—not just childbirth, but birth as creation and creative renewal. . . . [*Natality* is] an important and beautifully written read." —K.C. Compton, *Early Learning Nation*

"Jennifer Banks rightly affirms that Arendt's concept of natality is important for everyone, biological parents or not: Arendt challenges us to accept our agency, the possibility of the new, the insight that we're not born to die but to live. . . . Banks lays out questions that, if we follow them, might uncover wisdom that can inform mundane practice and policy alike to help us live well in such a world." —Sarah Beth V. Kitch, *Law & Liberty*

"*Natality* electrified me. It is one of the most perspective-altering, radical, empowering, and beautiful books I have ever read. It is strong and strengthening, brave and enlivening, and does what I am always hungry for, but rarely find—it enables us to think differently, newly." —Lucy Jones, author of *Matrescence: On the Metamorphosis of Pregnancy, Childbirth and Motherhood*

"A gripping exploration of some of society's biggest contradictions: our adoration for life but ignorance about birth, our reverence for mothers but disregard for their needs, and our focus on mortality but—until now—neglect of natality. This is a fascinating read."
—Dana Suskind, MD, author of *Parent Nation:*
Unlocking Every Child's Potential, Fulfilling Society's Promise

"Jennifer Banks has brought to light a dimension of experience that is both universal and weirdly neglected. This is a lucid, provocative, and groundbreaking book." —Christian Wiman,
Yale University professor and author of
My Bright Abyss: Meditation of a Modern Believer

"With poetic precision, Jennifer Banks moves deftly through various literary, living, and intellectual cultures to tell us about our beginning at a time when the gradient of most narratives dips toward our end. I will read *Natality* again and again to feel alive, to be reborn."
—Sumana Roy, author of *How I Became a Tree*

"To describe the revelation of Jennifer Banks's *Natality*, I find myself reaching for words like original, fertile, generative—words to describe not only the book but the way it acts upon you, and upon the world. *Natality* is a work of astonishing brilliance, beauty, hope, and generosity. I know I'll be buying it for everyone."
—Devorah Baum, author of *On Marriage*

NATALITY

NATALITY

*Toward a Philosophy
of Birth*

Jennifer Banks

W. W. NORTON & COMPANY
Independent Publishers Since 1923

For information about permission to reproduce selections from this book, write to
Permissions, W. W. Norton & Company, Inc., 500 Fifth Avenue,
New York, NY 10110

For information about special discounts for bulk purchases, please contact
W. W. Norton Special Sales at specialsales@wwnorton.com or 800-233-4830

Manufacturing by Lakeside Book Company
Production manager: Julia Druskin

Library of Congress Control Number: 2023952269

ISBN 978-1-324-07607-0 pbk.

W. W. Norton & Company, Inc., 500 Fifth Avenue, New York, N.Y. 10110
www.wwnorton.com

W. W. Norton & Company Ltd., 15 Carlisle Street, London W1D 3BS

1 2 3 4 5 6 7 8 9 0

For my family—
past, present, and future

The miracle that saves the world, the realm of human affairs, from its normal, "natural" ruin is ultimately the fact of natality.

—HANNAH ARENDT, *The Human Condition*

Contents

NATALITY

Introduction

Birth is humanity's greatest underexplored subject. I believed that when I started dreaming up this book thirteen years ago and I believe it still, although I have come to see how birth has been explored more extensively than I first imagined. Humans have thought about and written about birth from the beginning of recorded history, from ancient creation stories to medieval theological tracts, from philosophic manuals to obstetrics textbooks, and from nineteenth-century novels to twenty-first-century memoirs. Birth has been a preoccupation across cultures and eras, although its importance has waned and waxed like any other preoccupation, following the obsessions and anxieties of the day.

Look back at the earliest written sources and there birth is. Around the year 2300 BCE, the world's first identified author sang hymns to the goddess of childbirth, linking birth to creativity, midwives, divine powers, language, and her hope for change in the world. Ancient Akkadian poet and priestess Enheduana believed that this goddess of childbirth could move heaven and earth. "When she speaks, heaven shakes. When she opens her mouth, storms roar." The goddess's temple was like a mighty viper in the desert, Enheduana proclaimed, spreading fear. That temple had been built on a land of wrath. Glorious, huge, and beautiful, it mimicked creation itself.

Or in the *Rig Veda*, one of the oldest surviving texts in the Indo-European tradition, a voice throws out questions into a void, asking about the severing line between nonexistence and existence: what was above it, and what was below it? An ocean of emptiness was there, it tells us, a chaos in which desire sprang into being and planted itself in that vacancy, charged by some powerful, mysterious impulse. "Who can here declare it, whence it was born and whence comes this creation?" No answers are given. Written some 3,500 years ago, those questions still hover in the air.

In creation myths from ancient Egypt to ancient Greece, and from ancient India, Africa, and the Arctic to Indigenous communities in the Americas, the mystery of human birth was probed as a sub-narrative in the creation of the cosmos. Where did humans come from? How and why were they born? What is this creation they are a part of? The range and creativity of the answers people have come up with are astounding. The first humans are born from dismembered gods (Greek) or from the earth (Israelite). They emerged out of an ear of corn (Maya) or they were vomited out of a lonely god's mouth (Congolese). They are born by sex or without sex, with mothers or, more often, without any women at all.

But despite birth's recurring presence in the written record, and despite rumors of some long-lost matriarchal age and society that privileged a feminine divine and saw birth as the primary axis of imaginative, political, and social power, there is little evidence that birth was ever the foundational experience that any culture organized itself around. Just as women have been seen, in Simone de Beauvoir's phrasing, as "the second sex," birth has a sense of secondariness about it; it has long hovered in death's shadow, quietly performing its under-recognized labor. Death has been humanity's central defining experience, its deepest existential theme, more authoritative somehow than birth, and certainly more final. It is a given that humans are mortal creatures who must wrestle with their mortality, that death is the horizon no one can avoid, despite constant attempts at evasion and postponement and despite the recurring fantasy of immortality. Birth, meanwhile, is what recedes into a hazy background, slipping back past the limits of memory, existing in that forgotten realm where uteruses, blood, sex, pain, pleasure, and infancy constellate. Birth is a singular event, a succinct and contained vignette, and, unsurprisingly, it has been coded female: material, contradictory, messy, subconscious, sacrificial, sentimental, dangerous, powerful, weak, normative, subversive, and always lacking clear definition.

Perhaps it's a survival instinct: from the time one is born, death becomes the most pressing concern. How to avoid death, how to deal with it as an inevitability—these are urgent questions. Different traditions have defined a range of ways of confronting death and integrating that encounter into one's daily life. Roman Stoic philosopher Seneca spoke of death's omnipresence in our lives: "from the time you are born, you are being led to death." Our deaths are a point fixed by Fate; we cannot predict that point and we cannot control it. Accepting death and learning how to die were hailed by Seneca as paths to ultimate freedom. It is our love of life, he believed, our attachment to living, that holds us in bondage. "Study death always," he instructed. "It takes an entire lifetime to learn how to die."

Those who philosophize properly, Plato had asserted centuries before Seneca, are those who practice death and dying. In the Christianity that matured alongside such Greek and Roman influences, the crucifix would overshadow the manger as the central symbol of liturgical worship, with Christ's death and resurrection accruing more theological significance in most communities than Mary's miraculous birthing. Celibacy and an otherworldly asceticism would be recommended for those on the fast track to salvation; the end was imminent, many early Christians believed, and true seekers should seek not to perpetuate the human race, but to be reborn into God's kingdom. "Remember to keep death daily before your eyes," St. Benedict advised a faithful flock of celibate monastics in the medieval period.

Or, as Buddhists have insisted for millennia: to be born is to be chained to endless rounds of human suffering. The consequence of birth is death, a Buddhist maxim asserts, and the renunciant's goal is to escape from this hellish cycle, to gain enough insight into the nature of reality so that when a person dies, she is freed from birth once and for all. One ancient Buddhist text, the *Sūtra on Entering the Womb*, describes the uterus as a place where a body is trapped "amidst a mud of feces and urine . . . unable to breathe." The text is unambiguous in its perspective on birth: "I do not extol the production of a new existence even a little bit; nor do I extol the production of a new existence for even a moment. Why? The production of a new existence is suffering."

By the twentieth century, these philosophic and theological traditions would be reimagined by artists like Russian filmmaker Andrei Tarkovsky, who believed that "The aim of art is to prepare a person for death, to plough and harrow his soul." And by the twenty-first century, death was "having a moment," an *Atlantic* reporter declared, as millennials joined forces with aging baby boomers in the global death acceptance movement, creating "death cafés" and "death salons" where people could gather to discuss their mortality while sipping craft beers, eating cupcakes decorated with tombstones, and listening to presentations by hipster morticians.

But where are the birth cafés? And what hipster would ever be seen there? Faced with the resounding, final clap of death, what claims can birth have to existential, theological, or moral significance? To artistic or imaginative grandeur? To political importance? Does it really matter that we were born or how we were born, that someone carried us in a uterus and then ejected us into the world through a tight canal headed downward toward the earth, or that we emerged from an abdomen, or that we grew in some test tube? What was that process? Where did it begin and where did it end? How did it shape us and how did it transform the people and places we were born into? What is the place of birth in the widest and deepest human story one might tell? What, furthermore, is that story, and how should one honestly tell it? And what does it mean that the greatest power humans have had—the power to create another human being—has been relegated in nearly all time periods and all places to a secondary status, turned into a task to be performed by an underclass of people assigned that task on account of their gender?

I've asked these questions obsessively for over a decade. Birth often felt so huge and untamed, so morally dense and so imaginatively rich, that it continually overwhelmed all human attempts at naming it, controlling it, legislating it, limiting it, or mimicking it. It seemed to me like an immense and incomprehensible ocean, constantly moving and changing shape, ebbing and flowing, dwarfing the more stable land as it threatened and promised, damaged and created, pummeled its passengers unforgivingly and then lovingly rocked them to sleep. Birth was deadly, yes, but also brimming with colorful, never-seen-before life. Faced with the sea's turbulence, humans have by and large preferred the hard solidity of land.

But what, I've wondered, would human life look like if that ocean was taken as natural habitat? Imagine what a human would be if the philosophers' mortal instructions, questions, and observations were imagined in reverse, and if the poets, sages, intellectuals, and political leaders had made statements more like these:

- From the time we are born, we are being shaped by birth.
- Study birth always; it takes an entire lifetime to learn how to give birth or to come to terms with our having been born.
- The great philosophers are those who practice being born and birthing.
- Keep birth daily before your eyes.
- Birth is evidence of our freedom.
- The fundamental purpose of art is to process the strange, painful, and miraculous experience of childbirth.

Saints and messiahs, revolutionaries and inventors, artists and queens: they'd all be seen as people who once were born. We may die alone but we were never born alone, a fact that would remain obvious; all human individuality is relative. Our births were made possible by other people and were conditioned by the material world we arrive in, a world that is materially altered by our births. We exist in relation to the natural world, not in transcendence of it, and while we are agents in our lives, we are never really masters. Humans are fundamentally natal creatures, we'd remind one another, and throughout our lives we will be forced, whether we like it or not, to wrestle with our own natality.

But wait: *natality*? Is that even a real word?

o o o

I came across "natality" the year after my first child was born, a decade into the twenty-first century, eight years after 9/11, many thousands of deaths into America's War on Terror, and in the wake of the financial crisis of 2008. I was in my early thirties and was working as an editor at a university press about an hour up the coast from where I lived. Each morning I'd drop my daughter off at a small, cramped daycare, passing her into the arms of another woman. She'd wail as I walked down a corridor lined in finger-paint smudges on colorful paper, out through the heavy double doors and into the crowded parking lot. Fresh from the rapture, alive with birth's dizzying intensities, I'd drive alone up I-95, past factories and smokestacks, supermarkets and fast-food chains, ATMs and strip clubs, hugging the coast and gripping the wheel with a silent, anxious, maternal fury. A limb was missing. Who was she, back there with that other woman? And who was I now? What had just happened? I wasn't the person I had been. I thought the common things that many new mothers think after giving birth: *Why did no one tell me what this was like? Why did no one prepare me? Where was birth in all those books I've read so voraciously since childhood?*

An hour up the coast I'd go, into the outer world of meetings, conferences, opinions, and ideas. I'd park my car and walk past the Gothic Revival buildings lining the streets, interspersed with maple trees, past the castle-like library that sat magnificent at the center of campus, with its millions of books and underground tunnels. I'd enter my office, sit down, and start with emails, with the daily work of reading submissions from the world's leading experts on various subjects. There were books on just about everything, it seemed.

Everything except birth.

And then, there it was: "natality." One strange word, suddenly appearing in a book proposal I received from a philosopher who was writing on childhood. The term, the philosopher said, had been coined by Hannah Arendt, one of the most celebrated and controversial thinkers of the twentieth century, known for her work on totalitarianism and genocidal regimes. Natality conveys the idea that birth as a beginning represents (in Arendt's words) "the supreme capacity of man," a capacity inherent in human life that is the "miracle that saves the world, the realm of human affairs, from its normal, 'natural' ruin." Because we all were born, Arendt believed, we are always all capable of beginning again, of starting something new through each human action—the most prized of capabilities, in Arendt's estimation. These definitions had an immediate, powerful resonance, the philosopher said, because Arendt articulated them after fleeing Nazi Germany as a childless Jew.

The author casually mentioned natality and then moved on. But the word had ensnared me. *Natality*? Familiar words lurked within it—natal, native, nature, nativity, nation—and yet natality itself had an alien ring. Natality is in the dictionary, I discovered, but usually with a definition as brief as "1. birthrate." But Arendt wasn't speaking about statistics. Her natality planted itself in my imagination with all its foreignness and stayed with me, flowering in unexpected ways over the next thirteen years. In a world bedeviled by destructive tendencies, Arendt's creative and democratic approach to birth, her entirely worldly and simultaneously miraculous understanding of natality, had a strong, subversive appeal. In her own life, Arendt *chose* not to have children; natality was not pro-natalism, not an argument for why women should give birth or become mothers, or why a given community needed to reproduce. But she understood that while we may not choose birth, birth has already chosen us. That fact is inescapable. Natality works conceptually and broadly politically in her work, as a consistent and connecting if somewhat submerged theme, bringing together love, origins, revolution, tradition, the future, miracles, democracy, mistakes, forgiveness, imagination, happiness, freedom, and the common world of human plurality, among other topics.

Over the next thirteen years, I returned to Arendt continually, circling around, sinking in, and sometimes feeling alien in her definitions, as if I was watching birth from a hundred miles in the sky, noticing patterns I had been utterly blind to but somehow missing so many of the details.

I knew birth's details. I was living them. They came to define everything I thought about natality; birth's existential depths would be inextricably chained for me to the cycles of breast milk, sleep schedules, food preparation, and diapers. They weren't so biologically defined for Arendt, perhaps because she never gave birth, but also because of how she understood the biological realm as separate from the domains of culture and politics. Pregnant women, children, and mothers scarcely appear in her work, an absence I lamented, probably unfairly. My own sense of natality grew distinct from hers, but Arendt, in all her tenderness, perceptiveness, sense of irreparable loss, and even rage, showed me things about birth that no one else ever had.

I clung particularly to this insight of hers: that it is not enlightened wisdom to doubt human natality, or to argue against birth's crucial role in human life. It's a sign, rather, that one is ripe for totalitarian control. In the world today, celebrating birth can seem like an oblivious denial of just how dire our political, social, and ecological reality is. But Arendt saw birth and our engagement with it as a deep, direct encounter with reality in all its materiality and brutality, rather than as an evasion of it. What she detected in vari-

ous totalitarian movements was people's belief in their own "cynical
'realism,'" a conviction that their vague, expansive hatred—of the
world and of other people—was based on a realist reckoning with
the world, when in fact it merely expressed their complete alienation from reality. It's a stupid cynicism, she believed, that denies
birth's creative capacities—a cynicism that suggests one knows less,
not more, about reality and that tries to mask a deeper bafflement.
Totalitarian leaders, she wrote, know neither birth nor death and
"do not care whether they themselves are alive or dead, if they ever
lived or never were born." They take power when their subjects have
stopped caring too.

Totalitarianism thrives, she continued, in conditions where people are profoundly isolated from one another and "when the most
elementary form of human creativity, which is the capacity to add
something of one's own to the common world, is destroyed." Each
new thing we add to the world is another birth; our having been born
is what guarantees us the ability to act, to work as agents in our societies. Once that creativity, as she defined it—birth, politics, action,
people coming together to create new lives and new realities—had
been completely extinguished, you had a mass society of atomized
individuals who could be completely coerced into doing anything
their leaders ordered. They had lost touch with reality, a reality that
included the fact that they had all once been born and that this birth
was evidence of their inherent, miraculous creativity. "Ideologies,"
she wrote, "are never interested in the miracle of being."

As I was having my kids and editing books, I read about what
Arendt saw as an "unredeemably stupid fatality." I learned about
what the cynical, fatal masses had done to Arendt and her people, had done to themselves and to human civilization, and how, in
Arendt's words, the "whole of nearly three thousand years of West-

ern civilization . . . with all its implied beliefs, traditions, and standards of judgment, has come toppling down over our heads."

o o o

Although Arendt achieved fame as one of the most controversial
thinkers of the twentieth century, alternatively demonized and worshipped, "natality" never made it far outside academia. Natality was
virtually ignored by everyone other than specialists, and there is
still no single, alternative word to express for birth what "mortality" expresses for death: how birth shapes all human life, defining
its limits and its possibilities. Medical advancements have revolu-
tionized birth over the last century, and a simultaneous explosion
of writing and research about childbirth has been published in novels, poems, academic studies, how-to books, and memoirs across the
globe. But birth remains a niche topic, a singular event relevant only
to those experiencing it immediately.

The insights about birth developed by countless thinkers are
still not woven into everyday life. Most people who have spent time
with birth admit birth's seismic power, either positive or negative,
and acknowledge its great significance. They don't deny it, but they
often lack the language to articulate what it is or how it works. *Birth
is beyond language*, many people have told me. It's ineffable—too
mysterious and contradictory, too joyful and too tragic, too sus-
pended somewhere between irreparable loss and rapturous gain—to
be captured fully in words.

Even as birth is ubiquitous now—splashed on the covers of magazines, dramatized in reality TV shows, and graced with its own
product lines—it remains somehow shrouded in silence, exiled at
the farthest reaches of what can acceptably be talked about in polite
company. Motherhood and hospital stories of women in labor are
cloying, overplayed themes, I've been told. A book on birth would

only be for women and probably only for new mothers, I've been informed. Such women, a publisher told me, won't want to *think* too much about the subject. Implicit in that statement is the assumption that no one else would want to think about it either. And so I'd witness them, mothers gathered in private, sharing birth stories the way veterans share war stories, like a secret upon which a society depends but which lingers in its shadows. Birth was unthinkable, indescribable, quaint, graphic, sentimental, dangerous, exploitative, enraging, and downright embarrassing.

In ancient Akkad, the priestess Enheduana had described the goddess of childbirth as "the lady who imposes silence." Fast-forward 4,300 years and still: that resounding silence. In 1949, American poet and critic Muriel Rukeyser questioned the primordial imposition, asking, "Why is an absurdity felt here? And why is there a silence?" Why is it so difficult and absurd to talk about so large an arena of experience, such a complex and common group of meanings? When we look for birth, we are surrounded by great blanks. The fear of birth, the taboos around it, go so deep, she believed, that even the taboos cannot be named for what they are. "There is a terrible fear of birth abroad," she wrote. "It is close to the fear of poetry; and I do not know how closely it is connected with the agonies of our wars and with the daily crushing of the fiery life."

By the twenty-first century, not a lot had changed. The wars went on and the fiery life was crushed daily. Birth remained unspeakable. "Speech is a selfish act," Irish novelist Anne Enright wrote in the opening of her wry 2013 memoir about motherhood, "and mothers should probably remain silent . . . So I'd like to say sorry to everyone in advance. Sorry. Sorry. Sorry. Sorry." She says sorry to the people who don't like to read about birth, to the people who only want to hear about exceptional, dramatic traumas when it comes to birth, and to those who find her approach too intellectual. She apologizes for her insides and for being so ordinary, for joining the ranks of the smug and astonished. She fabricates the breaking headline "MARRIED WOMAN HAS CHILDREN IN THE SUBURBS" and admits that "it's not exactly a call to arms."

A book on birth, British novelist Rachel Cusk observed in her 2001 memoir about new motherhood, belongs not by the front door in the bookstore, but in that esoteric, rarely visited section "at the far end of recorded human experience, just past diet books and just before astrology."

o o o

In the twenty-first century, birth remains alien, lingering at the furthest astrological reaches, not only because of its graphic physicality, its bleeding carnal women, and its sexual explicitness, but also because of its thorough domestication and widely perceived tameness, its smug cuteness and its reputed role in conserving a mainstream, normative order, one controlled largely by men. Feminism grew up in the twentieth century partially through various women's radical disavowal of a traditional sexual politics that used birth as the key engine for women's subordination. A woman who wanted to do anything of significance in this life needed a "room of one's own," as Virginia Woolf famously put it, not a house overrun with children. Simone de Beauvoir went further, writing, "Woman has ovaries and a uterus; such are the particular conditions that lock her in her subjectivity."

Brilliant, radical, second-wave feminist Shulamith Firestone agreed with this point, arguing that women live "at the continual mercy of their biology—menstruation, menopause, and 'female ills,' constant painful childbirth, wetnursing and care of infants, all of which made them dependent on males . . . for physical survival." It wasn't just men who were to blame. It was nature itself. The biological division of labor had turned women into procreative birthers and that division marked the beginnings of all class and caste systems, she believed. It was the first inequality, and it led to "psychosexual distortions" which humanity is still wrestling with. Firestone imagined a cybernetic future in which technology would take over childbearing and the work of raising children would be distributed across a society's members. Childbirth, she believed, was barbaric, like "shitting a pumpkin." Artificial wombs would release women from the tyranny of this painful and laborious reproduction. Nature could be transcended.

Birth was understood as a problem by many loud voices in the movement, and sometimes their critiques of birth have overshadowed the complex and even unparalleled richness in birth found by many self-described feminists. The feminist critiques came as a needed corrective, and they deserved to be heard. Many women, after all, had died in childbirth since time immemorial. Women were given little agency or credit when it came to birth, but they were forced to deal with the full weight of its consequences. Birth ravaged women's bodies and foisted upon them heavy loads, limiting the paths open to them. Expectations about birth had essentialized women according to a set of often oppressive ideas about gender, leaving the nonconforming, infertile, non-procreating, and celibate at the margins. The problems around birth needed to be exposed.

The easiest way around birth's many conundrums was to avoid it altogether, to throw the baby out with the bathwater. Other movements in the twentieth century made this same recommendation on different grounds, adding fuel to the flames of feminist critiques of birth. A global population control movement, for instance, sounded the alarm about humanity's increasing numbers. There are too many people, Paul R. Ehrlich argued in his bestselling book *The Population Bomb,* first published in 1968. Population growth is a cancer that must be immediately excised, he believed, before we birth straight into our own oblivion. Mass famine was on the near horizon. "Hundreds of millions of people are going to starve to death," he anxiously predicted. Environmentalists have amplified and diversified the theme, documenting the hastening rate of extinction for nonhuman species in the Anthropocene. As environmental scientists have painfully illustrated, humankind is a destructive species, a threat to biodiversity. One of the major ways individuals can limit their carbon imprint, protecting other species, is by not reproducing.

By the twenty-first century, giving birth was not looking like a great option in many parts of the world. Having a child would limit one's career opportunities and it would drain one's finances, a serious concern at a time when safety nets, both governmental and familial, had dramatically eroded in many nations. Birth would hurt the environment and entail one's participation in gender inequalities. It would be a selfish act, some argued, in a world with millions of orphans.

Self-described "Birthstrikers" gathered into a small movement, refusing to have children and expressing their terror at the apocalyptic future any children might face. Natality rates are presently at record lows. About 44 percent of Americans between the ages of eighteen and forty-nine without children, both men and women, say they don't plan on having children at any point in the future; most of them simply don't want kids, they report, while about a quarter of them cite medical reasons and about 14 percent cite financial concerns. Rates have fallen across classes and age groups, among the native-born and immigrants alike. In the UK, fertility rates in 2020 dropped to about a child and a half per woman, a record low. Global fertility rates likewise plummeted from the 1950s on, with wealthy G7 nations Canada, France, Germany, Italy, and Japan joining the US and the UK at the head of the pack.

The declines may be a natural response to positive developments, including the fact that people in these countries are living longer and exercising more control over their reproductive lives. But the declines are accompanied by troubling and not unrelated trends: growing inequality and loneliness, rising suicide rates, fewer social services, greater political polarization, the spread of false narratives and propaganda campaigns, political setbacks for women, the stalled campaigns for racial justice, and the erosion of democratic norms. These phenomena all point to a profound isolation at the heart of modern life, a pulling back from a shared, embodied, and committed life with other people. Birth, like democratic politics, challenges us with otherness, with the putting aside of oneself to make room for another person, and with the challenges of difference and plurality.

The critiques of birth are not easily dismissed; without them, it is hard to imagine a different and more just social order. The negativity toward birth has had costs, however. It has historically alienated many ordinary women from the feminist movement, stymieing a more systematic reappraisal of gender relations and emphasizing the priorities of individuals against the needs of the collective, a tension that has long run through the women's movement. Discrediting it or declaring it barbaric means undermining many people's experiences and diminishing the role that women in particular have played in the history of human civilization. The aversion to birth that is articulated as an open rebellion against a patriarchal tradition often directly echoes the shame and disgust expressed about birth in patriarchal sources, creating an imaginatively closed feedback loop.

A barrenness haunts these visions of life beyond birth, but it also haunts the fetishizations of birth that can seem at first like affirmations of birth. In the twentieth and twenty-first centuries, for instance, birth has been used as a powerful moral prop by political movements otherwise deleterious to human life. In terms of political priorities, various pro-natal groups have valued the fetus's life more highly than that of the struggling mother or the hungry child, the sperm in the body of a man awaiting execution, the first-grader about to be gunned down in her classroom in a senseless mass shooting, or the species on the brink of extinction. Its activists wage their battles on behalf of the unborn. But what about the born? Why do the born in their accounts seem so doomed, so stamped with original sin upon emerging from the womb, that their lives no longer matter? In so exclusively sanctifying the unborn, these groups often approach birth as an unforgivable degradation. The pro-life concept of fetal personhood also erases birth as the transformative rite of passage it has long been.

What is missing in the culture war's heated, polarized debates are the voices that imagine other possibilities, those who intuit a freedom *in* birth, not *from* birth. These intuitions are very often best expressed by those who grasp the checkered history of freedom itself. There are countless people for whom the fight for reproductive justice is inseparable from a strong and unwavering commitment to birth and to life. Muriel Rukeyser, for instance, a single, bisexual mother, saw in birth a manyness, a plural people sending signals across vast differences, imagining new ways of living, unimagined values. Birth was not her trauma; her trauma was the forced hysterectomy she underwent after giving birth, because of her marital status and her sexual orientation. Or take American novelist Toni Morrison, a descendant of slaves and a single mom of two boys, who described becoming a mother not as the nail in the coffin of her oppression but as "the most liberating thing that ever happened to me." Or consider Indigenous American novelist Louise Erdrich, who admitted that not giving birth was a sensible choice for many, given the state the world is in, but who simultaneously praised birth as being "as original a masterpiece as death."

These are not the voices broadcast the most loudly in the public discussion about birth, where the lines are aggressively drawn, uncrossable, in arguments over abortion, immigration, population growth, and motherhood. The strict polarity of these debates denies how most people live—not in one bunkered ideological camp but in the difficult, messy, and conflicted moral ground between birth's extremities. Natality begins in that more neutral territory with a rather modest recognition: that we all were born and that our births indelibly shape human life from beginning to end. It challenges us to look at birth's full spectrum and diversity and to recognize how much we still do not know about what a human life is, what its parameters are, and what its relationship should be to other people and other life forms. Natality can show us how birth is relevant to all people, not merely to those asked to carry birth's heaviest loads. It starts from a place of observation and questioning rather than from any heated ideology. It is neither intrinsically pro-natal nor anti-natal. It doesn't automatically entail any statistical race to repopulate the world, or any pessimistic campaign for the extinction of the species, although it could, of course, lead those wrestling with it to either extreme position.

More than anything, engaging with natality is an act of the imagination—a deep dive past the limits of consciousness, a cognitive leap into what we can never remember and into the experiences of other people. It opens us to the vast range and limits, vitality and tragedy, beauty and ugliness of human life. It entails the practice of asking and of living birth's questions. "Be patient toward all that is unsolved in your heart," wrote Rainer Maria Rilke, a poet who circled repeatedly around the theme of birth throughout his career. He asked such questions as, "What keeps you from . . . living your life like a painful and beautiful day in the history of a great gestation?" Do not seek answers, Rilke advised. Instead, "try to love the questions themselves, like locked rooms and like books that are now written in a very foreign tongue." Birth has been a locked room, a book written in a foreign tongue, and engaging with natality is how we break into that room; it involves finally learning the foreign tongue constantly spoken in the background of our lives.

Minimizing birth means diminishing one of the greatest powers humans have had: the creation and sustenance of life itself, the bringing forth of a next generation that might live better, imagine more, suffer less, and create a more lasting world. This doesn't mean we need a specified mass of people, or that it's necessary to stay at replacement levels. Maybe we *should* dwindle down, dial back, and hold our own viral spread in check until we've found more sustainable ways to live on our planet. But I stop far short of extinction, alarmed by descriptions of our species as a scourge that must be wiped from the earth, portrayals that come close to those used to justify ethnic cleansing. I've hungered for a different set of principles, new models, a culture less reconciled to its own extinction. I keep imagining it: a society rooted in gestation, intimacy, vulnerability, growth, creativity, reciprocity, change, and otherness—in that strange and unrivaled symbiosis, the entering into the bloodstream of another human being.

o o o

Exactly who or what are people striking against when they go on strike against birth? There are other stories one might tell about refusals of birth, and it's easy to miss them. I've tried to listen in, discovering them far afield but also in the nearly inaudible whispers in my own home.

My husband, for instance, was born in 1972 in a small town in Gujarat, India, in the years when a Western-led campaign to limit the number of children that poor, untouchable people like his parents could give birth to reached its apogee. Despite having the youngest and the second-largest population on earth, India also has one of the world's longest-standing official family planning programs. In the early 1950s, not long after the nation gained independence, and while Western countries were experiencing their postwar baby booms, India adopted the world's first national policy aimed at shrinking its domestic population. Contraceptives, sex education, and, eventually, sterilization were aggressively offered to both men and women. Technologies that Western feminists had celebrated for furthering the crucial cause of reproductive choice were taken up by neo-Malthusians and eugenicists who saw in birth control, sterilization, and family planning a way to shrink burgeoning populations in other countries. India was a point of particular focus. The Western population controllers who went there and were welcomed by Indian leaders came home horrified by the country's crowds and by what they saw as its people's impoverished, unmitigated misery. Their concern was sometimes an expression of genuine humanitarian impulses, but very often it was also infused with nationalistic, eugenicist, and exploitative ambitions and driven by fears of marauding, non-white hordes. Controlling human populations became in the twentieth century an alternative to outright warfare, with other countries kept in check not by the military occupation of their land but by strategic social engineering schemes targeting their people's fertility.

In 1975, three years after my husband was born, Indian prime minister Indira Gandhi imposed a state of emergency, giving herself the power to rule by decree. Among the human rights violations that occurred during the Emergency was a campaign directed by Gandhi's sons that resulted in the forced sterilization of over eight million people in a single year—exponentially more people than were sterilized by the Nazis. The effort, bankrolled by American taxpayers, mandated that men with two or more children have vasectomies, and it also led to the sterilization of many men who were political opponents of the Gandhis or were poor, uneducated, or disabled. Botched operations killed thousands. The Indian people, still organized in loosely connected states distinguished by different languages, identities, and traditions, by and large resisted this centralized government program. Many of the family planning efforts in subsequent years shifted to the sterilization of women, who seemingly had less power to resist. But still, the campaign has been widely perceived as an abject failure. For a complex set of reasons, not all of them liberatory, many people in India kept giving birth, even when incentivized not to, and even when that birthing was an act of civil disobedience.

My husband's parents had no more children after he was born. As a Dalit man, was his father subject to forced sterilization? Was his mother targeted? If so, my husband suspects they would have welcomed the sterilizations, burdened as they already were with three children and limited resources. He was glad they limited their family to three children; he grew up knowing how hard it had been for his grandparents to have large families, how difficult it was for his parents even to raise him and his two siblings. But he also grew up

seeing the signs that read "Hum Do Hamare Do," meaning "We Two
Our Two." The message was clear: two parents should only have two
children. But there he was, growing up as a third child who violated
the generational symmetry, the human surplus that posters warned
against. This background has fostered my husband's discomfort
with group names like Birthstrikers.

The reality is that pro-natal norms have rarely been promoted
across populations. There have always been groups of people—the
poor, disabled, religious or racial minorities, women on welfare, the
gender-nonconforming, the sick—whom no government or powerful interests want to reproduce. People in these groups can come to
birth with different baggage, histories that ironically help them see
in birth opportunities denied to them in the broader culture: for
familial intimacies, self-definition, life affirmations, love, continuity
with and respect for their ancestors, creativity, and the creation of a
better world.

The pressure to procreate may feel real to many people, and
motherhood can be presented as an idealized state, but most mothers can attest to the fact that motherhood can be superficially championed yet more deeply undermined by their culture. Motherhood
is venerated in places like the US and the UK except when it comes
time to pay the bill from the maternity ward, offer maternity leave,
feed a mother's children, or come up with solutions to the childcare
conundrum. Birth goes against widespread cultural values in the
West: to accumulate and hoard capital, to seek one's own individu-
ation and success, to create and maintain one's own private space,
to avoid discomfort, and to eschew risk. Birth breaks down most of
the dualisms humans use to structure reality: man/woman, mind/
body, thought/experience, destruction/creation, self/other, creator/
created, birth/death. In challenging those binaries, birth can be an

act of nonconforming, and motherhood an expression of alterity. Therein lies the difficulty of talking about birth today: birth is both the norm and its transgression.

o o o

In *A Room of One's Own*, Virginia Woolf described the great difficulty women writers faced when they tried to set pen to paper in the early twentieth century. The problem was that they "had no tradition behind them, or one so short and partial that it was of little help . . . there was no common sentence ready for her use." Similarly, the problem today, when we try to think or talk about birth, is that we have no strong, synthesized tradition of wrestling with our natality to draw on, no common sentence about birth. Birth is fragmented into billions of individualized pieces, privatized and understood in the context of families, not societies. We have rich intellectual, existential, and spiritual traditions around birth, but they remain buried and are hard to access, leaving many to ask, "Why did no one tell me what birth was like?"

In this book, I sketch a version of this tradition, a lineage of people (mostly in the West, in modernity) who wrestled with their natality, and who derived great meanings from birth. They offer examples of how what people experience in birth and what they think about their experiences can shape their lives, deeply impact their societies, and even alter the course of history. They understood birth as a private event, individually experienced in people's bodies, but also as a stone thrown into a huge lake, creating broad social, cultural, and political ripples. Birth, they believed, was implicated in the sustenance and transformation of human civilization. Most of them recognized how birth had been misused throughout history, and they imagined a new relationship between birth and freedom.

I've focused on seven people I kept coming back to as I read and thought about birth: Hannah Arendt, Friedrich Nietzsche, Mary Wollstonecraft, Mary Shelley, Sojourner Truth, Adrienne Rich, and Toni Morrison. They are, admittedly, an odd, contradictory cadre— many of them rarely mentioned in the same breath—but they are also bound by hidden affinities, and they collectively constitute a submerged and surprising countertradition about birth's creativity in modernity in the West. They all leaned toward birth, either experientially or conceptually; they were passionately *for life*. But in being *for life*, they recognized birth's magnitude, great difficulty, diversity, and unresolved problems.

Living and writing on that thin but fertile path between cynicism and sentiment, they saw in birth a problem *and* a possibility. They understood birth as a life-expanding force that affirms and can renew human life, amid forces that aim to restrict it. They eschewed the dead end of anti-natalism, but none of them were pro-natalists, committed to some coercive race to reproduce. Most of them approached birth with an unorthodox, spiritual insistence that's irreducible to one political position, any dogmatic talking points, or any singular emotional register. They didn't perform that old sleight of hand: charging women with the impossible task of redeeming a fallen humanity, while not addressing the hard fact of their inequality. Birth wasn't for them the apotheosis of womanhood. But they also didn't see birth as something to be carelessly discarded, to be left behind in the pursuit of spiritual salvation or women's empowerment, and it didn't necessarily entail the passive reenactment of some script other people had chosen for the masses. It was haphazard, full of improvisation, of successes and failure, happiness and humiliation, and it always resulted in something unprecedented. Certain themes appear in their explorations: democracy, politics, action, god(s), gender, tradition, revolution, mothers, embodiment, change, poetry, nurture, love, and freedom.

In a series of portraits, I tell these writers' birth stories—their own births, their experiences giving birth or not giving birth, and their encounters with other people's births—but their stories are not all labors and deliveries, all hospitals, midwives, fetal monitors, or crowning heads. These are portraits of people wrestling with natality throughout their lives, exploring how their experiences with birth and their ideas about it shaped what they thought and how they lived. Natality requires a zeroing in on birth but also a zooming out, an exploration of birth's aftermath and the larger shape a human life takes. In order to grasp that overall shape, I have chosen people who are no longer alive and for whom biographical material is readily available, either through their own narration or thanks to the efforts of scholars, editors, and biographers.

The lineages I've mapped are idiosyncratic, based on my own evolving sense of birth as a nexus of human creativity. Each person's experience of their natality will be different; natality isn't a prescriptive grand theory, and I encourage readers to define natality for themselves, to map out their own lineages. This isn't a comprehensive or broadly representative study. There are major omissions, and the full intellectual history of natality remains to be written.

I think of the following portraits as, more than anything, a string of natal pearls, arranged poetically. Hannah Arendt once described poetic thinking using the image of a deep-sea diver plumbing the depths of the ocean in search of pearls. These pearls are subject to the ruins of time, she wrote, but the diver arrives to "pry loose the rich and strange," to bring it to the surface, into the "world of the living." This is what I have attempted: a deep-sea diving, a swimming through my intellectual inheritance, looking for birth pearls. I offer to readers what I found and most loved: a collection of the rich and strange treasures I observed buried alive. This is an invitation into natality. I hope that these poets, novelists, philosophers, activists, and political theorists can help us rediscover birth in our midst, imagine how it relates to the life of our societies, and challenge us to lean into the future against which our backs are pressed so hard and perilously.

—1—

The Miracle That Saves the World

Hannah Arendt was born in Hannover, Germany, on October 14, 1906, to a family of secular, left-leaning, prosperous Jews, at the beginning of what would be a cataclysmic century. She was "born on a Sunday evening at quarter past nine," her mother, Martha Cohn Arendt, wrote in a privately kept record she called "Our Child." "The birth took twenty-two hours and went normally. The child weighed 3,695 grams at birth." This happy birthday came just months after Martha's father's death; birth and death would collide for the Arendt family in the very same year. And Martha couldn't have imagined what would soon follow that successful delivery, those twenty-two hours of normal labor.

Arendt would become one of history's strongest theorists of birth, but we know little about her own birth, what that labor felt like in her mother's body. Her mother recorded birth's aftermath, however, with precision: the suckling schedule, weight gained or lost, the amount of milk ingested by her beloved child. Martha also kept a book that documented the birthdays, names, and deaths of those in both the Arendt and Cohn families, a source that provided her biographers with the main details of Arendt's childhood, and that suggests that Martha thought it was important to document their family ancestry, to anchor themselves in a very specific genetic history, with births and deaths acting as signposts. Martha Cohn had been born in 1874, shortly after the creation of the German empire and just before civil registrations became mandatory in all German states, at a time when births were tracked mainly by families and churches. From Arendt's earliest days through 1917, her mother diligently kept this diary, producing a private account of the early formation of a child whose adult, public life would become better known.

Arendt was born a Jew, she'd later emphasize. She didn't choose that Jewishness and she couldn't change it. So much of who we are is mysteriously given to us at birth, she believed: our "mere existence" and the fact of our inequality. We aren't all born the same. Biological birth isn't democratic or equalizing; it delivers us into the "abstract nakedness of being nothing but human," a vulnerable state that can be related to only through friendship, sympathy, or love. This kind of love, she'd later write, says, " 'I want you to be,' without being able to give any particular reason for such supreme and unsurpassable affirmation."

The Jewishness she was born into determined the direction her life would take. She would soon discover what happens when one has only the "abstract nakedness of being nothing but human," a humanity stripped of citizenship or membership in a defined community, and when one's givenness is not related to through friendship, sympathy, and the immeasurable grace of love. Anti-Semitism simmered in Germany when she was a child, although the full terror of the Nazi regime may have still been on the far horizon. But by all accounts, Arendt's parents wanted her to be, and they delighted in their newborn daughter, raising her in a warm, loving household where her existence was strongly affirmed. "The temperament is quiet but alert," wrote Martha. "We saw the first smile in the sixth week, and observed a general inner awakening."

As an adult, Hannah Arendt spoke little of her childhood. She divided her life into "Then" and "Now," a division whose parameters she would repeat and alter, as she lived through a series of dislocations and life-changing events. She was her parents' first child, and she would be their last. By the time she was two, her father's syphilis, which had been in remission, had come back, and when she was three, the family left Hannover and returned to Königsberg for his treatments. The capital of East Prussia, Königsberg was a garrisoned port city positioned on the Baltic Sea, far at the eastern end of the German empire, in what is now part of Russia. Long a center for Protestant learning and steeped in Lutheran history, it was populous, left-leaning, and culturally diverse when Arendt grew up there, with a strong Jewish community.

They returned to a large, extended, assimilated family that was well established in the city, moving into a roomy, comfortable house, but Arendt's memories of that time and place are shadowed by her father's illness. He entered a psychiatric hospital when she was almost five and she would visit him there, playing cards with him, until his dementia advanced to the point where he could no longer recognize her. Her mother reported that her daughter was "good and patient" with her father, praying for him every morning and night, but that she sometimes wished he simply wasn't alive any longer. By the time she was seven, he was dead. Arendt comforted her widowed mother, assuring her that such a loss befalls many women, and she cried at the funeral, "because the singing was so beautiful." Her biographer, Elisabeth Young-Bruehl, believed that Arendt's father's death brought a happy, rich childhood to an end, but her mother described her daughter still as a "sunny, cheerful child with a good and warm heart."

She was left in her generous and loving mother's care, surrounded by more women than men, women who so often outlived their husbands and children. Her home life, the happiness she experienced there and the warmth of those human relations, would be relegated by her to the private realm, a domain that must be shielded from the public gaze and that was entirely distinct from the political realm she would come to write about and occupy. Her home life was full of music-playing and storytelling, guests and conversations. Her mother noted Arendt's "acute capacity for observation" and her "burning interest in books and letters." She thrived as a young child, but she always had a strong sense of being an outsider—a feeling of uncanniness that she'd later understand as pariahdom, connected to her Jewishness and her long period of statelessness as a refugee, but also an innate consequence of her having been born. Birth turns us into newcomers, she'd later argue; we don't know the world we are born into, and the world doesn't know us. Life is a long process of getting acquainted with the world, and of that world adapting to us and to whatever we create within it. Her family assimilated into a largely Christian Germany, but her mother also taught her that her Jewish identity was irrefutable. If someone made an anti-Semitic comment in school, her mother instructed her, she should stand up immediately, march out of the classroom, come home, and report the incident to her mother who would promptly write a letter. She felt "absolutely protected" by her mother, who taught her how to maintain her dignity.

Born a Jew, she'd need to accept her own Jewishness in an increasingly anti-Semitic, Christian society, and she'd need to continually adapt to and be reborn alongside whatever history threw at her. The twentieth century's various conflagrations weren't foreseeable from the time of her birth, but she was born into tensions and conditions that would ultimately gather and make possible a disastrous alignment. Less than a year after her father's death, World War I broke out and Arendt and her mother were forced to flee on a packed, chaotic train to Berlin, where they stayed for ten weeks with family until the Russian forces had been defeated by the Germans. This was the first of a series of geographic dislocations that would be painfully repeated in Arendt's early adult years, and, in response to the war and its upheaval, she developed a series of illnesses and grew afraid of leaving home.

"It is almost impossible even now to describe what actually happened in Europe on August 4, 1914," she'd later write. "The days before and the days after the first World War are separated not like the end of an old and the beginning of a new period, but like the day before and the day after an explosion." After the explosion, even sorrow hadn't been able to set in, because the first explosion set off a chain reaction that would go on for decades. A baffled, cynical hatred of everyone and everything took root and radiated out in all directions. Decades later, she'd write that those deceptively quiet postwar years "assumed the sordid and weird atmosphere of a Strindbergian family quarrel." But how did she experience this atmosphere of disintegration as a child? How were those diffuse hatreds and "the cruel majesty" of the new order palpable to her, as a young girl? As she ran outdoors, read books in her dead father's library, and blithely sang off-key, she was being turned into the "scum of the earth"—an undesirable—by anti-Semitic propaganda.

She wrote poems and grew from a cheerful child into a disobedient, headstrong one. She was kicked out of school for leading a

student boycott of a teacher who had dared to offend her. In one of
the final chapters of "Our Child," Martha described her daughter as
becoming "difficult" and "opaque." A rift may have grown between
them, but she maintained her support for her independent daughter,
giving her the freedom to pursue her studies as she wished. Arendt
was a precocious, talented student and in 1924, at the age of seventeen, she matriculated at the University of Marburg, during a period
of relative, postwar stability. She was drawn quickly to a cultlike figure at the center of a philosophical rebellion against tradition: Martin Heidegger, her young, married professor with two sons. He was
for her the "hidden king," a magnetic presence. In him, "thinking
has come to life again," she later recalled. She was riveted.

Heidegger would become famous for his ideas about how we
are "thrown" into the world and how this thrownness results in
what he called our "being toward death." Because our lives are
finite and our deaths are unavoidable, an authentic human life
is oriented toward death's horizon, is lived in reference to it, he
argued. With natality, Arendt would eventually argue the reverse:
birth and the miracle of our creative beginnings are what indelibly shape us and prove our capacity to creatively act in the world.
She would come to reject key aspects of Heidegger's thinking,
but she was strongly drawn to him and he to her. In 1925, they
began a secret, joyful, and for Arendt bewildering love affair that
lasted until 1928, when he cut it off. She was heartbroken, but their
friendship endured, even after a seemingly unforgivable betrayal:
Heidegger joined Hitler's party while Arendt was fleeing Nazi
Germany for her life.

Some critics have seen natality as Arendt's rebellion against
her former professor, her Nazi lover—her mordant way of flipping
Heidegger the philosophic bird.

○ ○ ○

In photos of this period, Arendt looks pensive and bookish, shy but not lacking in confidence, as if lit by an inward self-assurance. Her eyes have an intensity that would deepen, sadden, and sharpen in the challenging years ahead, as she honed her powers of observation, staring down the unimaginable. After studying with Heidegger, Arendt pursued graduate studies at the University of Heidelberg, where she wrote a dissertation under Karl Jaspers that would be published decades later in English as *Love and Saint Augustine*. Already, she was working toward a theory of birth, although she would not gather her ideas into that single word—natality—until after World War II. Nor had she begun to think through birth's more political implications.

In the dissertation, she followed Augustine into what he called "the camps and vast palaces of memory." Birth is often associated with the future, but for both Augustine and Arendt, it is also in our past, individually and collectively, as a point of origin. Here she charted a very different course from twentieth-century Futurists like Filippo Tommaso Marinetti, who proclaimed, "Let's go, my friends! Let's leave! . . . We are about to witness the birth of the Centaur, and soon we shall see the first Angels fly." Marinetti rushed into the future, praising the "beauty of speed" and advocating for the demolition of museums and libraries, those mausoleums of the past. He was climbing out of the "Maternal ditch, nearly full of muddy water" and "bracing slime," all of which reminded him of "the sacred black breast of my Sudanese nurse." He was leaving that womb, that water, that woman, and that blackness behind, preparing himself "to glorify war." "We stand on the last promontory of the centuries!" wrote Marinetti. "Why should we look back over our shoulders, when we intend to breach the mysterious doors of the Impossible? Time and Space died yesterday."

Time and space had not died for Arendt, and they never would. Natality was no Futurist concept, and not only because of Futurism's self-described "burning and overwhelming violence," its intense misogyny, or the links between the movement and fascism. Arendt always kept history as a reference point. A world of future possibilities can only be created by reference to the past and a rooting in the present. This is for her the "triumph of memory": it deprives the past of its pastness, turning it into a future possibility. Our entering the world through birth is what establishes humans as conscious, remembering beings, people dependent on and involved with other people. This confrontation with our nonexistence isn't for Augustine or for Arendt a shattering of the self, a self-oblivion. Although humans may have been created out of nothingness, the fact that they were made at all paradoxically negates all forms of nothingness. "Once called into existence," Arendt writes, summarizing Augustine, "human life cannot turn into nothingness."

For Augustine, examining his own origins led to the insight that he had not created himself. In the place where others have perceived an utter absence, Augustine found his Creator, a Christian God. But for Arendt, a resolute belief in a Christian creator god would be a verity, like the verities of her ancestral Jewish faith, that had "lost all concrete relevance." She retained, however, respect for such beliefs, and the sacredness of origins would remain a key concept for her; without a sacred, creative origin, tradition and authority lose all meaning and therefore all power. Totalitarian regimes, she would later observe, thrive in times and places in which people have lost a shared set of meanings, a sense of belonging to a tradition.

Arendt grew away from Augustine and from theology, but her work was also a lifelong attempt to uphold that Augustinian belief that "once called into existence, human life cannot turn into nothingness." The Holocaust and her uprooting from her home would challenge her physically, intellectually, morally, and imaginatively in the years ahead. The loss of her home, her geographic origins, would reinforce and further develop these themes; they'd become more politically focused. Her most famous work, written decades later and published eighteen years into her statelessness, would also be about our search for origins. But this time the origin she sought was the constellation of forces that had tragically aligned in the twentieth century to make totalitarianism possible.

o o o

Much was lost in the years between those in which these two works were written. In Arendt's words, "It was as if an abyss was opened." Her early adulthood would be spent in flight, as a stateless person. These were her peak childbearing years, but they were experienced as a series of losses and ruptures. She'd marry twice but never have children. Although she wrote about birth, she almost never touched on motherhood, an experience she neither seemed to want for herself nor to encounter the right conditions for. At the same time, however, she'd remain close to her own mother.

As she finished her dissertation, at the age of twenty-three, the ground beneath her was shifting. The stock market crashed in New York and the economic situation grew worse in Germany, just as Arendt was trying to make a life for herself as a recent graduate. In 1929, she re-met Günther Stern, a Jewish philosopher with Communist sympathies, at a masquerade ball in Berlin. They moved in together, he helped her prepare her dissertation for publication, and they quickly married. With each passing year, however, she grew more political, aware of the increasing anti-Semitism around her, and she and Stern grew quietly and quickly apart. Arendt informed her disappointed mother of the strains in the relationship and told her that her marriage would remain childless. Stern, meanwhile, grew frustrated in his wife's shadow, describing her as "profound, cheeky, cheerful, domineering, melancholic, and always ready to dance."

By 1933, Hitler had come to power and the Nazis were rounding up German Communists. Stern fled to Paris but Arendt stayed behind, turning her apartment into a way station for escaping Communists and engaging in an information-gathering mission for the Zionists. One afternoon, she and her mother were brought into a police station for questioning. She spent eight days in jail before convincing her surprisingly friendly captor, a man with a sympathetic, decent face, to free her, and by outright lying about the activities she'd been involved in. Legality, she could see, no longer mattered. The German government had stopped allowing people to leave the country, so Arendt and her mother had to escape illegally to Prague, traveling on foot through deforested and heavily mined mountains, through a landscape of ridges, dams, and sinkholes with little other than birth, death, and marriage certificates and some of Arendt's writings in hand. They found entry into the country through an inconspicuous border station: a house with a front door in Germany and a back door opening east into Czechoslovakia.

That border crossing marked another break in Arendt's life, another painful rebirth. Observing how various intellectuals were voluntarily joining the Nazis, she felt isolated, surrounded terrifyingly by empty space. Was she looking down and back at Germany from those high altitudes, through rolling hills and scenic vistas? Or was she looking ahead into the unknown of a foreign country to which she would never belong? She left Germany between her past and future, gripped by the present, with a determined resolution: "Never again! I will never have anything to do with 'the history of ideas' again." In her passport photo from 1933, both horrified shock and steady recognition are written on her face; her arms are crossed loosely, and she holds a cigarette between her index and middle fingers. Her face, her clothes, her hairstyle, and the look in her eyes would all change in the years ahead, but for the rest of her life, the cigarette would remain right there, lodged between her fingers.

From Prague, she traveled to Geneva and finally to Paris, where she was reunited with her husband and joined a community of other émigrés. Among them was Heinrich Blücher, a working-class poet and philosopher, a Communist and bohemian anarchist who was known as a great talker. The two fell instantly in love, eventually divorced their spouses, and started living as husband and wife in a small hotel room. Their relationship was both intensely intellectual and passionately erotic. When she was away, Blücher wrote to her, "Do you realize that I am the man with the plumb that will sound your depths . . . the man who has the drill that will make all the vibrant springs of passion flow from you—the man who has the plow that will plow you so thoroughly, that all the nourishing juices within you will awaken?" He continued, "I want once more to be in the arms, between the legs, on the mouth, on the breasts, in the lap of my wife."

This was decades before the first birth control pills were authorized, and it's unclear how the couple avoided pregnancies after such steamy exchanges; I've found no mention of birth control methods, nor of missed periods, unplanned pregnancies, or abortions. Arendt and Blücher never had children. As she later explained to a friend, "when we were young enough to have children, we had no money, and when we had money, we were too old." Blücher offered a different explanation to his mother: "We decided not to have children in times such as these. We are sad about it, but a sense of responsibility for those who might be innocent sufferers is a valuable thing." Many of their émigré friends would also remain childless.

Perhaps stress helped the childless stay childless. World War II had begun, the French government was rounding up enemy aliens, and anti-Semitism was rising in Paris. Blücher was sent to an open-air Olympic stadium where he slept on the ground before being shipped to an abandoned château. After two months he was released, and they quickly married in a civil ceremony in Paris, but there would be no extended honeymoon period. Soon, they were separated again, and this time they were both shipped off, Arendt to an internment camp for women, Gurs, in the south of France—a large, swampy stretch of land crowded with identical makeshift cabins lined up in rows and surrounded by barbed wire, with bad food and no running water. Arendt witnessed there, over the five weeks of her internment, her fellow captives' wild fluctuations between suicidal despair and what she called "a violent courage for life." To survive the experience, many turned from the immediate terror of their situation, and that turn away from life as it was in the present into a remembered past or a hoped-for future was, in her mind, a disastrous betrayal of their humanity. In hope "the soul overleaps reality," she'd later write, and in fear it "shrinks back from it." As Samantha Rose Hill has argued, Arendt saw hope as "a dangerous barrier to acting courageously in dark times."

Eschewing hope, she expected the worst, and her pessimism may have saved her. In a brief, chaotic transition when France fell to the Nazis, she escaped alongside two hundred other women, carrying only forged exit papers and a toothbrush, and leaving about seven thousand women still interned behind her. She walked out alone, hiking and hitchhiking through the countryside in search of friends and family, with whom she was eventually reunited. By a stroke of luck, she and Blücher received emergency American visas, and they traveled to Lisbon and spent three months there before boarding a boat to New York. Her mother would soon follow. They settled in their new city, found work (Arendt worked briefly in Massachusetts as a housekeeper), learned English, and connected with other German émigrés. She wouldn't become an American citizen until 1951, after eighteen years of not belonging to any country and the denial of any basic political rights.

All these experiences dramatically shaped how she understood birth. Birth became less of an existential concept, as it had been when she wrote about Augustine, and an increasingly political, anti-totalitarian one. What's amazing to me is just how much her interest in birth survived these years of unfathomable loss and devastating betrayal, how she continually reimagined birth inside and alongside everything she experienced. Afterward, she infrequently talked about or wrote about these personal hardships, so it's hard to know what encouragement the prospect of new beginnings gave her day by day, how much her sense of her own natality kept her alive, anchoring her in the present, however dire its conditions. Some readers have been embarrassed by natality, by her talk of birth and new beginnings, not believing that she really meant any of it and perhaps considering the theme beneath her. But birth was consistently there in her work, an enduring preoccupation and an integral, undeniable, under-recognized theme. Birth was still with her after the war, when she would make the connections between birth and freedom, and as she eventually found one English word to bear the weight of all her insights: natality.

o o o

After fleeing to New York in 1942, Arendt and Blücher began reading reports of the extermination camps and Hitler's final solution, realizing with horror how close they had come to the gas chambers. Thousands of the women at Gurs ended their lives at Auschwitz.

Arendt began writing to try to process what had happened, to understand how the people she had grown up among and in many cases had loved had turned against other Germans, against her and her people. In 1951, her analysis of both the Nazi and Stalinist genocidal regimes, of their unprecedented form of power, was published by Houghton Mifflin as *The Origins of Totalitarianism*. The book laid the foundation for her subsequent fame.

Origins opens by stressing the "grimness of the present" and the themes of "homelessness on an unprecedented scale, rootlessness to an unprecedented depth." She described a world of anticipation, a calm in which hope had died and both nostalgic attempts to escape into the past and hopeful efforts to flee into the oblivion of a better future were in vain. The past was irretrievable, and the future was entirely unpredictable. Humankind was living between desperate, reckless hopes and desperate, reckless fears. The world felt incomprehensible, and yet to yield to this sense of complete and utter disillusion of meaning was to embrace an existence that was "lifeless, bloodless, meaningless, and unreal." Meaning and life, blood and reality coalesced, coming together for her in birth and beginnings.

The shock of World War II is still fresh in the book's pages as she tries to make sense of the deadly convergence of anti-Semitism, racism, alienation, resentment, imperialism, nationalism, displacement, a crisis of political legitimacy, and the rapid technological change that spurred all these forward. "Never has our future been more unpredictable," she wrote, and "never have we depended so much on political forces that cannot be trusted to follow the rules of common sense and self-interest—forces that look like sheer insanity, if judged by the standards of other centuries."

Alongside this shock, however, is a strange surprise: the gratitude she expresses for the historic apocalypse she has just lived through in that it brought to the surface and made undeniable streams that had run subterranean below European life for millennia. The Holocaust was not a freak of human history, some wild, twentieth-century, German exception to human thought and experience, she argued. The situation was actually much worse. The Holocaust was a consequence of a death drive that ran deep through Western societies, one that had propelled humanity into a fruitless, barren place. Thought and experience had long ago parted ways, creating the conditions for radically distorted ideas about reality to take root in people's minds and setting the stage for a modernity in which people were alienated from one another. Locked in their own privacy, flying into their inner selves, they had lost faith in their ability to transform their worlds and to create new, plural realities through their actions and their speech. People survived in modernity only by setting their gaze elsewhere, outside the world into ideal abstractions or into some immaterial, heavenly hereafter.

The problem for modern man was the "irritating incompatibility" between his ability to control his reality—to create it, challenge it, or re-create it on exclusively human terms—and the impotence he increasingly felt as his powers vastly grew. Modern man was hamstrung between omnipotence and powerlessness, and he was bred to be either an executioner or a victim, with no nuances, no gradations in between. The Nazi and Stalinist regimes had tried to destroy their way out of the impasse; they flourished amid mankind's frustration at arriving at a place of mastery from which humans paradoxically and increasingly felt they had no agency.

o o o

But birth confounds the binary. It is an experience of neither mastery nor powerlessness; it confronts us with our embodied, earthly creativity, with what we can control and with what we simply cannot control.

Arendt works birth into *Origins'* analysis of the deathly machinery of totalitarian terror. In the very last paragraph, she concludes soberly but with a cautious sense of resilient promise that "every end in history also contains a new beginning." Here is her often-quoted passage:

> This beginning is the promise, the only "message" which the end can ever produce. Beginning, before it becomes a historical event, is the supreme capacity of man; politically, it is identical with man's freedom. *Initium ut esset homo creatus est*—"that a beginning be made man was created," said Augustine. This beginning is guaranteed by each new birth; it is indeed every man.

In seeing how the twentieth century's totalitarian regimes were neither unprecedented nor inevitable but grew out of specific conditions and the actions of individual people, she discerned a small seed of hope: a different beginning was always possible. This beginning could be as horrible as the birth of Nazism, but it could also be a renewal of human dignity, freedom, community, and democracy. Humans retained their agency; they could be active citizens, building a new world order. Their births guaranteed them this ability to act.

She'd revise the ending of the book three times. Did she really believe this: that a new beginning could be made, that humankind existed for this making? Although she wavered on how to conclude the book, the theme of birth and new beginnings would not disappear in her work. Birth was central to the ideas she developed in the decades that followed, as her career flourished and she settled into life as an American citizen.

o o o

Arendt's next, most highly celebrated work was *The Human Condition*, and in it, she more explicitly developed natality as a foil for the death drive of the totalitarian powers. She used that specific word "natality," trying to capture in one word the idea that humans "are not born in order to die but in order to begin." We aren't just mortal creatures; we are also natal creatures, born into human bodies and destined to live our lives out on the earth.

The book begins with a discussion of the otherworldliness she saw as a dangerous denial of our humanity. She had just observed Sputnik, the launch of a man-made object into an outer space no man could inhabit. This milestone in the race into space had been widely celebrated, she observed, as a step in the direction of human-kind liberating itself from its imprisonment on the earth. It was a triumphant "rebellion against human existence as it has been given, a free gift from nowhere," and an attempt to exchange that existence for something humans had made and could exile from Earth.

She saw the same basic problem in scientific experiments to create life in a test tube: that humans' attempt to create and con-trol life would only further alienate them from life as it is bodily experienced. The earth, she believed, is "the very quintessence of the human condition." Science itself wasn't the problem; the prob-lem was that scientific advances had outpaced the human ability to think about what science revealed. Science had allowed people to escape the bodies they had been mysteriously born into and to exit the earthly realm even as they still lived on the earth, in those birth-given bodies. Secularism had exacerbated the disconnect. She warned that the consequential turn from God the heavenly Father could be followed by a more fateful repudiation of Earth the Mother.

This was an intensifying quandary, but the dilemma, again, wasn't exactly new. The intellectual tradition she was heir to had long before been hollowed out by a pessimistic turn away from the material world with all its pleasures and problems, its plurality and mistakenness. Intellectuals' privileging of a contemplative other-worldliness had since Plato been driven by a critique that saw the world as somehow too contaminated by human action—its mess-iness, error, and unpredictability—and that believed the material domain was somehow less real than the ethereal realms of abstrac-tion and ideas. "The primacy of contemplation over activity," she argued, "rests on the conviction that no work of human hands can equal in beauty and truth the physical *kosmos*, which swings in itself in changeless eternity without any interference or assistance from outside, from man or god." "The more man learned about the uni-verse," Arendt continued, "the less he could understand the inten-tions and purposes for which he should have been created." This confusion caused him to doubt what he saw, to lose trust in his own perceptions and thus in any actions that were responses to those per-ceptions. That paralytic doubt replaced what the ancient Greeks had described as a shocked sense of wonder at the miracle of being alive, an enraptured feeling of being plugged into reality. Man began to suspect that he "is not, cannot possibly be, of this world even though he spends his life here." This confusion drew him inward, and he became a student of his own self, a tireless investigator of his own consciousness. This "innerworldly asceticism," as Max Weber called it, was a withdrawal from the world, but it was also what allowed man to possess the world, to claim it as his own, and it became "the innermost spring of the new capitalist mentality."

Arendt disavowed the disavowal of the world. She turned from philosophy, which had been powerless to stop the Nazis' rise (and in many cases, like Heidegger's, had sustained and buoyed Hitler and his totalitarian project), to politics. Politics had been responsible for the devastations, too, but politics held a promise for her that phi-losophy did not: the promise of the re-creation of human plurality.

Politics challenged her to soberly commit to *amor mundi*, a love of the world that actively resisted totalitarian nihilism.

Arendt's turn to politics was also a deepening commitment to the theme of birth, from which she drew increasingly strong political implications. "Natality," she wrote, "and not mortality, may be the central category of political, as distinguished from metaphysical, thought."

Birth was political because it was connected to the human, creative capacity for action. Each action is a little rebirth; it is haphazard, unprecedented, spontaneous, and surprising. It sets in motion a series of events and other actions we cannot foresee. Action is therefore risky; it is subject to human mistakenness, and it can go wrong. It is messy and inherently plural; we act together, not alone. It can't happen where there isn't the expectation of forgiveness because our actions are riddled with errors. But without action, nothing new would be created and humans would be trapped. Humans' capacity for action and for new beginnings is what guarantees them the possibility of freedom. Action is conceived through some combination of human agency and miraculous grace, and it breaks us from the prison of paralysis. She wrote in *The Human Condition* of how the new "always appears in the guise of a miracle." Man's ability to act "means that the unexpected can be expected from him, that he is able to perform what is infinitely improbable" and "with each birth something uniquely new comes into the world."

Arendt tried to separate birth from reproduction, which meant for her distinguishing action from labor. Labor, as Karl Marx had understood it, was the same life process as "begetting." For Marx, she wrote, "Labor was . . . the 'reproduction of one's own life' which assured the survival of the individual, and begetting was the production of 'foreign life' which assured the survival of the species."

This observation was at the root of Marx's theory of the modern age, one that echoed what both the Hebrew Bible and the classical tradition had long ago testified to: how labor is "intimately bound up with life as giving birth." *Be fruitful and multiply*, the Hebrew Bible authors had written, an injunction which rooted the ancient Israelite community on the earth, in nature's cycles of creation and depletion, birth and death, labor and consumption. This fertility was connected to what Arendt called "the sheer bliss of being alive which we share with all living creatures." A great happiness can be found in the process, in living in nature, in giving birth as mortals who will not live long, to other mortals who may outlive us but will ultimately die too. Humans can experience pleasure in this perpetual cycle.

But this cycle can also be imprisoning, Arendt believed. It amounts to being locked in one's biological metabolism. Marx himself had understood this and had failed to reconcile the main contradiction she identified in his work: that the laboring, begetting fertility he understood as so powerful was also what he wanted to transcend, to free humans from. Arendt was trying to work out a different solution to this problem: that our natural fertility is our great creative power, but in it is also our extinguishment. She found freedom not in biological labor but in action, not in reproduction but in birth, which she saw as a radical break in nature's regenerative cycle rather than as its perpetual spinning. Action and birth produced something new, rather than the same old seasonal crop, the endless ancestry of begats and begats. The birth of a human was no mere recycling of the biological materials that had existed before him, but a miraculous, unprecedented beginning.

These arguments would put her at odds with the radical feminists growing up and coming into consciousness at that time, with those who believed that biological labor and birth could not so easily be separated. To separate birth from labor in this way was to take it out of women's bodies. *The Human Condition* was published in 1958, at what was a peak for generational setbacks for the women's movement. That was roughly a decade into the baby boom, a postwar generational explosion Arendt doesn't mention and never took part in, but which hovers in the background of all she wrote about birth in those fruitful years of painful reckoning. The baby boomers were young enough to be her children or even her grandchildren, and many of them would see birth quite differently.

o o o

Arendt's natality began in tragedy, but it grew waveringly into a more pleasurable appreciation of birth's regenerative energies and of reality itself. "There is no lasting happiness outside the prescribed cycle of painful exhaustion and pleasurable regeneration," she wrote in *The Human Condition*. This pleasure is part of our worldliness, our existence as mortal creatures bound to this earthly home and its given set of conditions, however dire. "Pleasure," she wrote, "is fundamentally the intensified awareness of reality." Not even the fact that we can be destroyed takes away from this "tragic pleasure." Such a pleasure springs, she wrote, "from a passionate openness to the world and love of it."

Arendt was offered a new beginning, a rebirth, in America, and she made the most of it. Although she'd understand herself as unassimilated—a "conscious pariah"—she also embraced her new home, its political traditions, and the opportunities they offered her. She taught, lectured, and published widely in the postwar years, and her career flourished before her death in 1975 from a heart attack. She was sixty-nine. She and Heinrich Blücher had a long, happy, and strong marriage; their friends affectionately referred to them as the "dual Monarchy." She also had, as a friend remarked at her funeral, a "genius for friendship" and she stayed close with a group of émigrés she affectionately called her tribe. Her apartment was full of friends, laughter, and conversation. She enjoyed her worldly pleasures, cigarettes and cigars, Campari and sangria, parties and vacations, doughnuts and racks of lamb. Her friends have attested to her wonderful sense of humor.

Even amid a series of controversies and periods of intense ostracism, Arendt wrote about *amor mundi*, a love of the world. It became an integral theme as she wrote about birth and new beginnings, as she healed from the traumas of World War II. But her love of the world wasn't separate from the cataclysms she had experienced; it was rooted in the complete loss of the world she had known and the exceptional, unexpected miracle of any grace and pleasure that came after it. She took little about her new life for granted. She saw her aliveness as a miracle, an infinite improbability that obligated her to the world. Do "we love the world enough to assume responsibility for it," is the question her work asks. By taking responsibility for it, we can "save it from that ruin which, except for renewal, except for the coming of the new and the young, would be inevitable."

Although she never had children, the child would be an important figure in Arendt's work, even if it was abstractly defined. She treated this figure with all the anxious, loving tenderness her mother had shown her as an infant. She wrote that our faith in and hope for the world found "its most glorious and most succinct expression in the few words with which the Gospels announced their 'glad tidings': 'A child has been born unto us.'" She explicitly links the phrase to the Gospels, but in her development of natality, the child is not only Christ. The child is each of us. We were all once that newborn child. She reminds us of our own beginning, our own ability to start something new. The glad tidings aren't that we'll be whisked away to heaven when we die, but that creation is here within us, waiting for us to begin again in this haphazard, hazardous "festival of life." We are each a potential savior.

In all her explorations, birth was more than a singular, medical event we experience and then move past without sustained reflection. Birth was instead an ever-presence—a deep, imaginative well we can draw on continually. Birth taps into life's fresh and ever-running waters and is accessible to all people.

Arendt remains a riddle for me: a devoted daughter and obsessive of birth, who never gave birth and never paid much attention to mothers; a writer who turned away from philosophy, attending to a material present, but whose work was written at a philosophic remove; a stern, formidable presence on the page who was known in her life as a humorous and passionate friend, daughter, and lover. We missed each other in time; I was born two and a half years after she died, into a world she seems to have eerily anticipated. Across the expanse of the last century, I keep almost seeing her, imagining her, standing amid the twentieth century's bombed-out rubble with her eyes wide open. She is fiddling with the latch on birth's closed door, attempting to open the gate onto the full grandeur, frightening fragility, strange mystery, and astonishing creativity of human life.

—2—

The Soil Is Still Rich Enough

When Hannah Arendt's mother was still a toddler, learning how to walk and talk, a young German professor was working on a strange and arresting series of books that would help shape her daughter's consciousness. As Arendt grew up, she would read his books closely, decades after they were written, and she would wrestle with many of the same questions he had. How do we make sense of our lives in the context of crumbling religious certainties? What are human freedom and human agency? What alternative exists to the world-denying traditions modern Europeans are heir to? What is life itself and how should we cultivate it? As they tried to answer these questions, both thinkers put birth at the center of their explorations.

Friedrich Nietzsche is often thought of as a nihilist. But Nietzsche, Hannah Arendt argued, was no nihilist. She was born six years after his death, and she would be left to work through what she saw as his failed demolition of a death-centered Western inheritance. What Nietzsche cared about, she could see, was "power and life and man's love of his earthly existence." He had tried to put birth in the place where death had been in Western culture since antiquity, to affect a radical transvaluation. He imagined what human life would look like if birth, instead of death, was life's organizing horizon.

Nietzsche had famously announced God's death, writing, "God is dead. God remains dead. And we have killed him." But he saw that death as a beginning, not an ending. God's death created an opportunity for humans to turn away from the afterlife, from the alluring prospect of eternal life after death, toward the earthly, embodied life that comes after birth. Imagine it, he challenged his readers: we can immerse ourselves in this earthly existence, accepting our natal and mortal embodiment and even celebrating it. A new spiritual tradition can grow up around birth, life, creativity, sexuality, and procreation. He saw himself as the herald of this newborn tradition and, in his later years, he was its messiah.

Nietzsche believed that birth would be central to the revitalization of a godless world, the re-enchantment of a decadent society smoldering with petty resentments and paralyzed by a lifeless anomie. But it would take time for humanity to realize this. Unfortunately, time was running out. Eventually the soil would be depleted, unable to nurture any trees. The clock was ticking on humanity, but there was still a little time left on creation's watch. The "soil is still rich enough," he argued, and the "time has come for man to plant the seed of his highest hope."

But what exactly was that highest hope? What exactly did Nietzsche hope would be born or reborn? Was birth just a metaphor for cultural and spiritual renewal, or was he actually talking about the birth of new human beings? Nietzsche would die a single man with no children, a man whose imaginings grew increasingly hostile to women—the people doing the actual birthing all around him—

even as the creation, sustenance, and flourishing of real, embodied, mammalian life were held as his highest values. His philosophy built toward this bold and vexing assertion: "That there may be the eternal joy of creating, that the will to life may eternally affirm itself, the agony of the woman giving birth *must* also be there eternally."

Nietzsche passionately wanted life to go on, for humanity and for himself. But Nietzsche was his father's only surviving son and the Nietzsche family line would biologically end in him. As an unmarried man he had no women to give birth for him, and as a man he could not give birth himself. He theorized or perhaps fantasized about "male mothers," about a "motherly human type" that wasn't exclusively female and that did not fit neatly into existing gender categories. But his fatalistic peers could not recognize a creative, pregnant, overflowing artist like himself, a man who was trying to give birth immaculately to humanity's future. He was ahead of his time; he was one of the "premature births of the coming century."

Unfortunately, he did not live to see this century, and the problem he identified remains with us: that for human life to survive, "the agony of the woman giving birth *must* also be there eternally." This is a problem both for the men, who cannot give birth, and for the women, who must suffer such agony on behalf of humanity. Friedrich Nietzsche had no biological children, but he gave birth to books that wrestled with natality. He also spawned generations of intellectual heirs who have discovered him as Hannah Arendt found him: a man who smashed the mortal existential order he himself was heir to as a modern, white, educated, European man, but who left behind only a rough draft of natality, an exuberant draft that was full of its own irresolution. He left much—too much, perhaps—to the imaginations of his warring interpreters.

o o o

Friedrich Nietzsche was born on October 15, 1844, the first child of a newly married couple living in Röcken, on the outskirts of Leipzig, which was then part of Prussia. His mother was the sixth of eleven children of her pastor father, and at age seventeen she married a man thirteen years her senior. Young, pretty, warm-hearted, her face enlivened by intelligent eyes, she got pregnant mere months after marrying and gave birth at the age of eighteen. Her husband, the Lutheran pastor of a parish in Röcken, personally christened his newborn son in his parsonage, a building set alongside a medieval, fortresslike church, one of the oldest in Saxony. Nietzsche's younger sister would later capture the blessing in her written account of her brother's youth. "That which I am experiencing today," his father proclaimed, "is the greatest, the most wonderful event, yet, I am about to baptize my little infant! Oh thou blessed moment, oh unspeakably holy work, be blessed in the name of the Lord! . . . My son, Friedrich Wilhelm, this is how you shall be called on earth, in memory of my Royal benefactor, on whose birthday you were born."

The parsonage still stands. Nearby a gray stone church is surrounded by verdant grass, slightly overgrown, and a handful of pink roses. As a child, Nietzsche paid great attention to the willows, the flowers, but also to the gravestones in the cemetery. He listened to the church bells ringing on Easter Sunday, celebrating the resurrection of a dead, crucified human god—a god whose birth is at the center of the religion he still believed in.

His father, a dedicated royalist, named Nietzsche after the reigning king of Prussia, imbuing him with aristocratic potential. But Nietzsche was born into a family dominated by a triumvirate of women on his father's side—two doting aunts and his paternal grandmother, an "uncompromising materfamilias." Despite the strong, maternal, and womanly embrace, he was captivated early on by warlike male heroes. He loved to tell the story of how his own father had been born mere days before a major battle, near the ground where Napoleon was defeated. Where one was born and when one was born mattered, Nietzsche could see from an early age.

The family welcomed a newborn girl two years later, and in 1848 a baby brother was born. The family was growing, happily expanding. Those births were revolutionary in that they transformed the family, but they were conservative in that they cemented his father's role as paterfamilias and reinforced his commitment to the prevailing social, religious, and political order.

A change, however, was in the air that blew through their streets. The year 1848 saw the March Revolutions in Germany and throughout Europe—the Springtime of the People, as it was sometimes called, the most extensive revolutionary wave in European history. These revolutions were anti-monarchical, driven by democratic, participatory demands, and they spread like brushfire. Ordinary people took to the streets. Nietzsche's father's adulation of kings and his faithfulness to the church and its hierarchy were not shared by many within the German Confederation, the political successor of a shattered Holy Roman Empire. The map of Europe was being redrawn and disruptive ideas—democracy, liberalism, radicalism, nationalism, socialism, feminism, freedom of the press, and universal male suffrage—were gaining ground. Nietzsche's first memory was of German peasants in wagons waving celebratory red flags in this springtime of the people.

The Nietzsche family did not participate in these celebrations; his father was outraged by the rabble and was horrified that the king after whom he had named his son was capitulating to their demands. Meanwhile, the family's private springtime of the people, the happy era of the children's births, was quickly turning into a deathly winter. Nietzsche's father was prone to mysterious, sporadic paroxysms that left him suddenly unable to speak, staring blankly into space, having seemingly lost consciousness. His condition was diagnosed as a "softening in the brain." His son would remember him as "delicate, kind and morbid, as a being that is destined merely to pass by—more a gracious memory of life than life itself." By July of 1849, a year after his third child was born, Nietzsche's father was dead, at the age of thirty-five. Nietzsche, aged four, watched his father being buried, "committed to the womb of the earth." "When a tree is deprived of its crown it withers and wilts," Nietzsche wrote at age thirteen, recalling his father's death, "and the tiny birds abandon its branches." "All joy vanished from our hearts and profound sadness overtook us." Six months later, he dreamed of funeral music emanating from a church, and he saw his father emerge from his grave in a linen shroud, wander into a church, and come out with a baby whom he carried back to the tomb. An infant child who had emerged full of life from a woman's body was buried in his father's dead arms as a tiny corpse. The following day, his two-year-old brother very suddenly died, reopening the half-healed wound of his father's death.

Following those two "hammer blows from heaven," Nietzsche grew up in his mother's care, adored by her and his younger sister, Elisabeth. He later described a happy childhood, one rooted in the verdurous richness of the natural world. His recent biographer Sue Prideaux wrote of the "liberty and lightness of being that brother and sister found in their seemingly limitless playground, encompassing the church tower, the farmyard, the orchard and the flower garden." Another biographer, Julian Young, described young Fritz as a "precocious, shy, affectionate, pious, virtuous and obedient boy" who experienced the support of a happy and loving family. Despite the pleasures of the flower garden and the support of his loving family, his early losses haunted him. Natality and mortality, birth and death were wound inseparably in his early consciousness, as were male and female archetypes. As he explained in one of his last books, "I am . . . already dead as my father, while as my mother I am still living and becoming old." He was a father and a mother, both dead and alive; his ancestors lived and died in him.

The fatherless family would soon move from the parsonage, the "father-house," as he called it, into more cramped quarters, leaving the orchard, the flower garden, and the limitless playground behind. They relocated to bustling, more urban Naumburg, then at the heart of the Awakening movement, which prized passionate revelation over rationality. The family kept itself apart from the born-again revivalism, finding it too fanatical and favoring a more rational spirit. But Nietzsche was fervently drawn to the religious celebration of birth that takes place at Christmas. From a young age, he loved Christmas intensely, even more than he loved his own birthday. As a thirteen-year-old, he explained that Christmas is "the most blessed festival of the year because it doesn't concern us alone, but rather the whole of mankind, rich and poor, humble and great, low and high. And it is precisely this universal joy which intensifies our own mood." Christmas universalizes what is often experienced only individually: human birth. Although Nietzsche eventually rejected Christianity, he continued to be moved by Christmas and its ritual celebration of a "universal joy."

As a young boy and teenager, Nietzsche threw himself into his studies rather than into any revolutionary movement. He had an early passion for both literature and music, and he was a gifted and disciplined student. His mother wanted him to follow in his father's footsteps, into the church, and, after matriculating at the University of Bonn in 1864, he moved in that direction, pursuing studies in theology, which he ultimately found uninteresting, and philology, focusing on texts from antiquity. The parallels with Hannah Arendt's fatherless, maternally centered, German childhood and theologically inflected university training, although set a half century apart, are striking.

But Nietzsche had doubts: about the Christian God, and about his future as a philologist, despite his early and very promising professional successes. He rebelled, partaking in the intolerable "beer materialism" he critiqued in his fellow students, growing a little beer belly of his own, engaging in a duel, visiting a brothel, dressing as a dandy, and refusing to accompany his mother to church. He rebelled intellectually as well, turning against his father's Protestantism. For Protestants, he wrote, the "earth is a place of exile, the body is a prison. We must be filled with hate and disgust towards life. Man experiences a terrible urge to self-destruction." He began conceiving a new imaginary, one in which the earth was home, the body was a site of freedom, human existence was delightful, and self-creation superseded self-destruction. The purpose of philosophy was not, then, to prepare one for death, but to teach one how to survive and how to live. He wasn't quite ready to pioneer this new philosophy on his own, however; he needed a new guru, a new master—a God who was not outside the world, but *in* it.

A few weeks after his assumption of a professorship at the University of Basel, in 1869, he went to visit Richard Wagner, one of the most famous composers in Europe. This would be one of the most formative encounters of his life. Over the next three years, Wagner, his mistress Cosima, and Nietzsche formed a fateful, impassioned, and highly creative triumvirate. Some of the most iconic cultural works of the nineteenth century were produced by Nietzsche and Wagner during this period, as they imagined the rebirth of their society and the redemption of the world. While living on this "island of the blessed," as he called their time together, Nietzsche finished his first book, which focused intensely on the theme of birth: *The Birth of Tragedy*, a reimagination of birth in artistic and pagan terms.

A less observed fact about this triumvirate is that it was childbirth that first sealed the trio together. The time they spent together on their island of the blessed was also the creatively charged aftermath of the birth of a baby boy.

o o o

When Nietzsche first met Wagner, the composer was already among the most celebrated artists in Germany. He would become known as an ultranationalist and anti-Semite—ideological proclivities that drove an ineradicable wedge between him and Nietzsche—but he began his artistic career in the revolutions of 1848, the revolutions in the hazy background of Nietzsche's earliest memories. Wagner had manned the barricades in the streets, and a revolutionary spirit would infuse his work from its beginning to its more conservative end. He penned early essays with titles like "Art and Revolution" and "The Artwork of the Future." Art must regain its metaphysical value, he believed. He imagined his masterworks being performed at festivals for ordinary people, festivals like the ancient Greek fertility rites that were infused with regenerative possibilities.

Nietzsche was welcomed into Tribschen, Wagner's opulent manor house on Lake Lucerne, by the composer himself, in the first of twenty-three visits over the next three years. Wagner would have an outsize influence on his life and work, but the composer's mistress Cosima, who later became Wagner's wife, made an equally large impression. Nietzsche worshipped them both.

On Nietzsche's second visit to Tribschen, Cosima was eight months pregnant with her fifth child, her third with Wagner and his first and only son. Nietzsche was apparently oblivious to the pregnancy or thought little of it, and he was likewise unaware of what happened that night until he was informed of it the next morning by Wagner. Cosima went into labor at 3 a.m. Her cries echoed loudly through the house's pink, heavily damasked, and exalted halls. Midwives ran and up and down the stairs, making a ruckus that Nietzsche apparently slept through. Wagner roamed restlessly in and out of the laboring room; Cosima grabbed his arm as she writhed in pain, before instructing him to leave. He listened anxiously to her labor from a neighboring room, until finally, it happened: a son, Siegfried, was born as dawn broke and the sky filled with bright colors. Wagner wept. Cosima saw the boy as a "good omen," binding her lover more tightly to her. Wagner in turn believed Nietzsche's arrival had been fateful, that he owed his son's birth to the visiting professor, whom he came to see as his son's "guardian spirit." Wagner named his son after the hero of *The Ring of the Nibelung*, the operatic cycle he was then finishing: a hero charged with redeeming the world and one, strangely, whose mother dies giving birth to him. Cosima, fatefully, lived.

Cosima, for all her cool and cerebral distance, embodied the closest encounters Nietzsche would have with the raw and full physicality of childbirth (after, of course, his own birth). His visits to Tribschen were full of conversations about music, myth, and philosophy, but they were also populated by young children. Nietzsche played with Cosima's children, staged Christmas plays for them, painted Christmas nuts gold with them, brought them puppets, hid Easter eggs for them to hunt, picnicked in their company, and stared out the windows at the inspiring natural tableaux in which they were vivid, fluctuating features. He was often charged with babysitting duties, and he became a part of the Wagner family. He even was given his own bedroom in the house.

Cosima described her household as a "confusion of genius-creating, children-confusion, people relaxing noisily, animal-idolatry, etc." The household included "a governess, a nurse, five servants, two dogs, several cats, a peacock and a peahen," a horse, and "numerous cows, chickens, and sheep." Even long after he grew away from Wagner, Nietzsche remembered this overflowing house as the place where he felt most at home. Its chaos was his refuge. That chaos birthed him; without his experiences there, he would have been a "still-born creature," he later confessed to Wagner. Near the end of his life, he reflected on those "days of trust, of cheerfulness, of sublime accidents, of *profound* moments." His delight in Tribschen's crowded chaos sits in jarring opposition to the ascetic isolation of his later years.

The idyll was interrupted when France declared war on Bismarck's Prussia. Nietzsche joined the war effort as an ambulance attendant. He left for the front in high spirits, eager to serve, but was almost immediately undone by what he saw. The war, which lasted only six months, was a veritable bloodbath, and Nietzsche would never wipe its horrors from his consciousness. Contracting an array of diseases—severe dysentery and diphtheria were diagnosed—from the soldiers he attended to, he came close to dying. He was traumatized by Bismarck's fatalistic, culture-destroying militarism and philistinism and by the corpses of his countrymen strewn all around. The war caused a break in him; it set him face-to-face with the reality of human violence, a reality he would spend the rest of his life trying to both accept and sublimate. His military service bred in him a lifelong hatred of warfare, and it committed him to the goals of world peace and the abolition of war. Like all the suffering he experienced, however, it spurred him creatively forward. In a letter to a friend, he lambasted the war's "bloody soil" and confessed, "I am prepared for the worst and at the same time confident that here and there in the mass of suffering and of terror the nocturnal flower of knowledge will bloom."

o o o

A year and a half later, Nietzsche's first book, *The Birth of Tragedy*, was published. An exploration of classical Athenian tragedy, it was also a deep dive into the nature of human creativity, into birth as the apotheosis of that creativity. The book begins in pessimism, at a moment when "all man can now see is the horror and absurdity of existence." A nihilistic and anti-natalist sense of horror and absurdity is captured succinctly in the pithy, bleak statement of a wise old man. Nietzsche re-narrates the story of King Midas, who hunts down old Silenus, the ancient Greek god Dionysus's companion, and asks him what is the best thing for mankind. Silenus responds: "Miserable, ephemeral race, children of hazard and hardship, why do you force me to say what it would be much more fruitful for you not to hear? The best of all things is something entirely outside your grasp: not to be born, not to *be*, to be *nothing*. But the second-best thing for you—is to die soon."

At that moment, "in this supreme menace to the will," Nietzsche writes, "there approaches a redeeming, healing enchantress—art." Art assumes a role not unlike that of beginnings in Hannah Arendt's work. Both are about birth, the creation of something new.

Dionysus, the Greek god of the earth, fertility, rebirth, and the grape harvest, is the representation of this creative drive. Nietzsche says that if we turned Beethoven's "Hymn to Joy" into a painting, we would be close to the Dionysiac. There, all the barriers between men break down and he senses a "mysterious primal Oneness." This is a mystical union, an original cosmic womb. This oneness, this primal pregnancy, is full of suffering, but it is also infused with a celebratory exuberance, an "unbounded lust for existence and delight in existence" that is a crucial dimension of natality.

Nietzsche didn't invent the connection between birth and Dionysus; in classical Greek myth, humans were first born out of Dionysus's body after he was dismembered by the Titans. Dionysus was described as male, but he exemplified qualities that have long been perceived as female: darkness, chaos, disorder, irrationality, fertility, and earthiness. Dionysus stands for all that falls outside the bounds of conventional society; he is the foreigner and, very notably, the god of joy. He is associated with freedom and radical liberation. For Nietzsche, Dionysus is the anti-Christ—more primal and powerful, more life-affirming than any morality.

The Apollonian, in contrast, belongs to the powerful Greek god Apollo. Apollo is "'the shining one,' the deity of light." If the Dionysian represents chaos, the Apollonian represents order. The Dionysian is passionate feeling and the Apollonian is abstract reason. Darkness and light, female and male, stranger and citizen—Dionysus and Apollo were opposites, held in relation to each other. The Apollonian is illusory and it is what makes possible our belief in our separateness, what Nietzsche called the "wretched belljar" of human individuality. The Dionysian is closer to experiences like conception and gestation, to the confusion and joy of bodies growing together. Tribschen, for instance, was a Dionysian household.

In *The Birth of Tragedy*, Nietzsche argued that Athenian tragedy had perfectly balanced the Dionysian and Apollonian, giving the ancient Greeks a model for how to immerse themselves fully in life, with all its polarities and contradictions, its joys and its suffering, its births and its deaths. The death of Athenian tragedy in antiquity and the domination of the Socratic reason that came after it had, he believed, drained the Western tradition of the primal, joyful fertility that had fed the ancients and made them love their lives. Christianity with its otherworldly emphasis on the kingdom to come followed after Socrates. Nietzsche saw Christianity as "the embodiment of disgust and antipathy for life . . . a yearning for nonexistence . . . fatigue, sullenness, exhaustion, impoverishment of life." He hoped that in shining light on ancient tragedy, he could give his own culture a model for its own joyful rebirth.

○ ○ ○

Cosima and Richard Wagner read *The Birth of Tragedy* when it came out. They delighted in it, infused as it was with the creative, natal spirit that had charged their time with Nietzsche on the island of the blessed. But most readers did not share their delight. The book received a few terrible reviews and was otherwise met with virtual silence. Rather than birthing great artistic successes for Nietzsche, it coincided with the unraveling of his once-promising academic career.

Nietzsche remained highly productive after the publication of *The Birth of Tragedy*, but these weren't easy years for him. His books were commercial and critical failures and he suffered increasingly from a variety of debilitating ailments: frequent fevers, migraines, nausea, vomiting, insomnia, coughing, diarrhea, faintness, exhaustion, seizures, cramps, hemorrhoids, and deteriorating eyesight. His declining health made it impossible to keep up with his teaching and administrative responsibilities, and at age thirty-four Nietzsche retired. Desperately searching for a climate that would alleviate his symptoms, he ghosted his way through a series of rented rooms in various European cities, coasts, and mountains, becoming a nomad and experimenting with a range of ineffective and sometimes quackish cures. Intent on avoiding overstimulation and on funneling all his energy toward his creative projects, he increasingly withdrew into solitude. In between bedridden stretches, he took long, solitary walks in the mountains, exertions which gave him hours to think, gain perspective on the world, and draw inspiration from nature. He would return to his desk and a burst of creative energy would explode onto the page. Some of his major works were written in a matter of weeks.

For the rest of his life, he oscillated between health and sickness, a cycle both regenerative and depleting. As Sue Prideaux described it, "During each fleeting recuperation the world gleamed anew. And so each recuperation became not only his own rebirth, but also the birth of a whole new world, a new set of problems that demanded new answers." Julian Young guesses that Nietzsche may have been manic depressive. Nietzsche himself described his experiences in bipolar terms; health was an alpine height and sickness was a valley depth; his hikes and his descents, his health and his sickness, had given him access to a "*dual* series of experiences," an "access to apparently separate worlds." He had a doppelgänger, a second face, and perhaps even a third.

Despite his poor health and depressive stretches, he was possessed by a relentless, frenzied quest to renew culture, to restore his society to communal, cultural, and spiritual health, and he was convinced that he himself had to be the agent of that renewal. No one else was up to the task. His relationship with the Wagners soured as he struck out on his own, spurning the tutelage of his once powerful master and mistress.

Solitude fed Nietzsche, but he was still "human, all too human" and his very human desire for companionship had not entirely abated. Around the time he was finishing *The Gay Science*, the book in which he announced the death of God and imagined a love of one's fate that was so all-encompassing that one became a "yes-sayer," an affirmer of all of life, he met the ravishing Lou Salomé in Rome. Their meeting would spark a triumphal rebirth that soon led him to despairing, suicidal depths.

Upon meeting the aristocratic, Russian-born twenty-one-year-old, he exclaimed, "From what stars have we fallen together here?" "From Zurich," she succinctly replied. Sixteen years his junior, she would attract the romantic attention of some of Europe's most famous intellectuals. Her beauty was matched by her intellect and Nietzsche instantly fell in love, believing he had found both a disci-ple and a soulmate. She in turn was drawn by his intense eyes, which she saw as protectors of some great treasure. She sensed in him a "deep inner life" and "an almost feminine mildness." They took one long, magical walk together up Monte Sacro in the northern Italian Alps, discussing God and their deep spiritual yearnings. They may have kissed there; neither of them would ever tell. Nietzsche would describe that alpine hike as one of the most profound and exquisite experiences of his life. "Monte Sacro—" he told Salomé, "the most delightful dream of my life; I owe it to you." Although he was a critic of marriage, he proposed to Salomé multiple times. She rejected each proposal, determined not to marry or have sex because she did not want children. Children would lock her into a traditional female role, she knew, and she wanted her freedom, a chance to develop her mind. The pair nonetheless made plans to establish a countercul-tural, free-spirited, intellectual, and spiritual commune in an aban-doned monastery with their friend, the physician and philosopher Paul Rée. There the three would form an unholy but celibate trium-virate, they decided, and together they would build a new temple—a temple of joy.

As they made plans, Nietzsche excitedly revealed to Salomé his idea of the eternal return. He had begun to play with it in *The Gay Science*, and he would further develop it in his next book, *Thus Spoke Zarathustra*. What, he had asked in *The Gay Science*, would you think if a demon approached you in "your loneliest loneliness" and told you that you had to be perpetually reborn and relive your life over again innumerable times, exactly as you lived it the first time? What would you say to that? "Would you not throw yourself down and gnash your teeth," he asked, "and curse the demon who spoke thus? Or have you once experienced a tremendous moment when you would have answered him: 'You are a god and never have I heard anything more divine.'" Could we love our lives so entirely, he wondered, that we'd be willing to be infinitely reborn?

It's not clear what Salomé thought of his idea and, sadly, their plans for an unholy triumvirate quickly unraveled. Nietzsche's controlling and increasingly anti-Semitic sister intervened, intent on getting her brother away from Salomé, that "immoral" woman, and Rée, that "Israelite." Rée, meanwhile, had fallen in love with Salomé, who seems to have lacked any romantic interest in Nietzsche. Rée and Salomé fled, leaving Nietzsche heartbroken. He returned to his mother, his eyes swollen from crying, hating his sister for the intervention, and grieving the loss of his sensual, spiritual soulmate. But his mother only castigated him for the whole affair, calling him a "disgrace to his father's grave"—a grave, again, that had haunted him since he was a child. He started taking large doses of opium to dull the pain and help him sleep, and he hinted in letters about suicide. His ideas of greeting everything with an ecstatic yes, of loving one's fate, and of the beauty and joy in an endless return, would be put to their severest test. He looked at his life and saw a black sorrowful sea. "Alas, this pregnant nocturnal dismay! Alas, destiny and sea! To you I must now go *down* ... down deeper than ever I descended—deeper into pain than ever I descended, down into its blackest flood."

Very alone and very angry with women in these years, he grew increasingly and perhaps paradoxically toward Dionysus. If he had tried to hold the Dionysian and the Apollonian in balance in *The Birth of Tragedy*, evenly weighing male and female principles, in his later works Dionysus started to take over. A fertile, primal life force asserted itself against all systems, all order. Nietzsche began calling himself Dionysus, god of rebirth, newly incarnate and come back to renew the world. Was this just mischievous role-playing, or was something less whimsical going on? His friends who received letters signed "Dionysus" weren't sure what was happening. As he worked through the repercussions of the death of God, did Nietzsche start to believe that he himself was becoming a god?

However drugged and disordered he was in these years, his thought still followed an internal logic. God's death necessitated a new understanding of human beings, one that charged them with newborn powers. God hadn't simply been done in by infirmity or old age, after all. God had been murdered, and not by some devil or warring deity, but by the humans he had created as his own beloved children. This murder created ethical, spiritual, and existential problems for humanity. On the one hand, if humans could murder their own creator, this must testify to their great power. On the other hand, how would they live with this magnificent creative power in their own hands? Who would control that power? And how would they make sense of their lives? How had they been created and for what purpose other than to survive?

Nietzsche's sense of human power grew in reverse proportion to his personal and professional failures. The more he failed, the more his idea of what he called the superhuman (or *Übermensch*) developed. The Übermensch, often translated as the superman, was an evolved person who had courageously made his own way in the world, creating new values and defining new freedoms. Living in the wake of God's death, the Übermensch would give birth to a new world. In *Thus Spoke Zarathustra*, a book Nietzsche considered his masterpiece and a self-described "blood-letting" that exploded into his consciousness in the years after Lou Salomé left, he tried to connect the death of God, the Übermensch, and the eternal return, all through a fictionalized account of the historical Zoroaster. The book, written and published as four separate books over three years in the 1880s, is hauntingly and strangely filled with references to birth, procreation, pregnancy, nursing, sex, wombs, heirs, and children. Nietzsche saw it as the founding text of a new religion.

The book opens with Zarathustra, a saintlike figure who comes down from his mythic mountaintop, speaking about the Übermensch, a human who would step into the vacancy left by God's death, a leader who would commit to earthly life and to humanity. He would be a bridge, connecting past and future, redeeming past generations and justifying those in the future. He wouldn't just *take* risks, he *was* a risk; he himself was a rope thrown over a huge abyss, a "dangerous across, a dangerous on-the-way, a dangerous looking-back, a dangerous shuddering and stopping." Life, Nietzsche believed, was dangerous. It entailed existing in the very "belly of being." Those afraid of its primal chaos faced a more terrible danger: that of becoming dead ends, last men, creatures who did not create anything, did not birth any new beings. The people who birthed new children would outlast themselves and would create the future. A child represented humanity's highest hope for its survival.

His language about birth is confusing and contradictory; it's both metaphorical and concrete, euphoric and pessimistic. At times, he makes clear that women are the ones who get pregnant and give birth. "Man and woman," he wrote, "the one fit for war, the other fit to give birth." Giving birth is powerful, creative, liberatory, and redeeming. To have children is to play an active role in the unfolding of time. This fact seems to charge women with superhuman power. Such creative, birthing women need only a seed from a man to act as procreators, cultivators, and sowers of humanity's future. "Everything . . . about woman has one solution," says Zarathustra, and that solution is pregnancy. "Man is for woman a means: the end is always the child. But what is woman for man?"

The fact that this great procreative power belonged to women presented Nietzsche with two major problems. Not only was he *not* a woman and therefore couldn't bear children; he also didn't *have* any woman to do that bearing for him. So how would he give birth? In the third section of *Thus Spoke Zarathustra*, he heartbreakingly repeats the following lines seven times: "Never yet have I found the woman from whom I wanted children, unless it be this woman whom I love: for I love you, O eternity!"

Marrying himself to eternity, Zarathustra imagines himself pregnant. But he isn't pregnant with a human child. He is giving "birth to lightning bolts." He is full of milk, waiting to be suckled. His soul is the "umbilical cord of time." Men are creators and they can give birth too. Can't they? But what would they give birth to? Zarathustra suddenly turns on birth: "Whoever has to give birth is sick; but whoever has given birth is unclean. Ask women: one does not give birth because it is fun . . . You creators, there is much that is unclean in you. That is because you had to be mothers. A new child: oh, how much new filth . . . whoever has given birth should wash his soul clean." It is lines like these, among many others, that have earned Nietzsche a reputation as a misogynist.

But Nietzsche's reputation as a misogynist is somewhat checkered. He imagined a human more complex and multilayered, more devoted to life in all its manifestations than one singular, exclusive, and aggressive gendering can capture. Even the Übermensch is not entirely the exemplar of a hyper-masculinity that it might seem. The Übermensch, Zarathustra explained, would go through "three metamorphoses of the spirit." The spirit must first become a camel, stoically carrying all heavy loads (not unlike a pregnant woman). Then the spirit must become a lion, a brave, heroic beast who slays dragons and creates new freedoms, new values. But the metamorphosis does not end there, in slaying and leonine and perhaps masculine strength. The spirit must finally become a child. "Why must the preying lion still become a child?" Zarathustra asks, and then responds, "The child is innocence and forgetting, a new beginning, a game, a self-propelled wheel, a first movement, a sacred 'Yes.' For the game of creation . . . a sacred 'Yes' is needed."

Humans could still say a sacred yes to creation, birthing themselves forward in time, but their time was running out. "I say unto you: one must still have chaos in oneself to be able to give birth to a dancing star," Nietzsche wrote, with tumultuous depths and uncanny insight. "Alas," Zarathustra dimly prophesied, "the time is coming when man will no longer give birth to a star." If humans don't embrace their own chaos and give birth, sacrificing themselves for the earth and the next generation, giving themselves away in that act of creation, there will be only a dead end, a degenerate last man, a species with no new beginnings. Those who don't cross over, becoming a bridge between past generations and those in the future, pursue the goal of self-preservation. This is a futile goal, Nietzsche believed, as the individual self can never be preserved. Once one stops giving birth, there are no more bridges connecting the atomic self, no connecting ropes thrown dangerously across existence's empty abysses.

But Zarathustra is no last man. He has children. "Speak to me of my gardens," he begs, "of my blessed isles, of my new beauty . . . For this I am rich, for this I grew poor; what did I not give, what would I not give to have one thing: these children, this living plantation, these life-trees of my will and my highest hope!" The book ends with Zarathustra singing about a thirsty, hungry, terrible joy—a joy for all eternity—as he waits for his children: "My children," he says, "are near, my children."

These must be some of the most heart-wrenching lines ever written by a lonely, middle-aged, childless man.

o o o

Nietzsche's mental state and health deteriorated in the years after *Thus Spoke Zarathustra* was published, but this was also a period of artistic crescendo, of frenetic productivity. Over the Christmas season of 1888, he took a dramatic turn for the worse. On January 3, 1889, after a year of unmatched creative output and increasingly erratic behavior, Nietzsche broke down when he saw a coachman ruthlessly beating a horse on the street. Overwhelmed with compassion, the story goes, he started sobbing and ran to the horse, wrapping his arms around its neck. In *Thus Spoke Zarathustra*, Nietzsche had presented pity as his hero's final test; he would need to overcome pity. But Nietzsche himself could not overcome pity. After witnessing the horse's beating, he descended into a psychotic, delusional state. He screamed, paced, drank his urine, smeared his feces on the walls, and slept on the floor. His communications were fragmentary and nonsensical. Doctors diagnosed the source of the breakdown: syphilis, contracted during a visit to a brothel in his youth. Scholars since have doubted this diagnosis, and the true cause of his madness may never be known.

His breakdown was sexually and perhaps manically charged. His doctors wrote that "the patient asks often for women" and observed "a high state of manic excitement. Considerable priapic content." His sexual arousal was continuous with the philosophic themes he'd been intently exploring in the months before his psychotic break. In *Twilight of the Idols*, written on the brink of madness and published twenty-one days after the horse-beating incident, he offers one of his most succinct definitions of the Dionysian, a definition that is full of birth and female sexuality. The Dionysian was:

> The triumphant Yes to life beyond all death and change; *true* life as the over-all continuation of life through procreation, through the mysteries of sexuality . . . Every single element in the act of procreation, of pregnancy, and of birth aroused the highest and most solemn feelings. In the doctrine of the mysteries, pain is pronounced holy: the pangs of the woman giving birth hallow all pain.

These are extraordinary lines coming from a man who lived celibately for most of his life.

Nietzsche composed a few bizarre and stunningly beautiful letters in the weeks immediately after the break; these were the last things he ever wrote. Sometimes called the "Letters of Insanity," they are signed, alternatively, "The Crucified" / "Nietzsche" / "Dionysus." It is as if the three identities had merged in his own self-understanding. He was the dead, crucified god; he was himself, Friedrich Nietzsche; and he was Dionysus, the god of rebirth. In one letter, he goes so far as to say that "at bottom I am every name in history." In his insanity, he had achieved the unification of all souls that he had long dreamed of. He continues with this astonishing assertion: "With the children I have put into the world too, I consider with some mistrust whether it is not the case that all who come *into* the kingdom of God also come *out* of God." Nietzsche likens God to a birthing mother, a powerful entity who brings forth children out of herself. Is this the God Nietzsche believed he was becoming?

Nietzsche spent the last decade of his life guarded and paraded around by his sister, Elisabeth Förster-Nietzsche. After a string of her own personal failures, including the disintegration of a colony she had founded in Paraguay with her virulently anti-Semitic husband (who, drowning in debt, had killed himself), she saw an opportunity in her brother's break. It came just as Nietzsche's literary star was rising. She seized control of his estate and began the decades-long project of editing and publishing his work, in order, many scholars have argued, to reflect her own nationalistic and anti-Semitic values. She founded the Nietzsche Archive, which became a fascist hangout. Nietzsche died in the summer of 1900, tragically never benefiting from the fame he achieved late in life, but also never living to see the full, terrible flower of Nazism or the role his work and family played in it. He missed his sister's breathless letters praising the Führer: "At the head of our government stands such a wonderful, indeed phenomenal, personality like our magnificent Chancellor Adolf Hitler."

o o o

Nietzsche is not widely thought of as a great philosopher of birth. Generations of readers and scholars have focused on concepts such as the Übermensch, the will to power, and the death of God, rather than on Nietzsche's deep engagement with natality. But natality—its sparkling promises and its intractable contradictions—simmers on nearly every page of his work.

Nietzsche wrote many uncomfortable things about women, leading some to brand him an antifeminist. But feminists have held mixed opinions of him. An early advocate of women's admission to universities, he maintained close relationships with women and with specifically feminist women throughout his life, including after his heartbreak over the Lou Salomé affair. Women played many roles in his life: mothers, grandmothers, sisters, confidants, conversation partners, inspirations, tormentors, lovers, betrayers, and prostitutes. He was no steadfast proponent of women's rights or advocate for women's liberation; his work in fact insisted on hierarchies, on the fundamental inequality of all people. He emphasized human difference, not as an expression of individualism but as an aspect of human community. Each member of a community must play their designated part, he believed. For women, this often meant having babies to perpetuate the human race. It's not hard to see how many women have resented being assigned this role by a childless philosopher as he hiked alone through Europe's snowy peaks.

Nietzsche was, however, uniquely attuned to problems and experiences that had long been understood as exclusively female. In paying such close attention to birth, he attended to a subject that many other philosophers considered irrelevant or beneath them. Perhaps he belonged loosely to that nebulous tribe Louise Erdrich was thinking of when she wrote, "We owe some of our most moving literature to men who didn't understand that they wanted to be women nursing babies." He bore clear-eyed witness to the inequality women were subject to. He understood how the women of his day were expected to give themselves away, to submit, while men were supposed to possess, to master. A man who loved without this sense of possession was not considered a man. Those expectations hadn't helped him much, and such love had done little for women. "This wild avarice and injustice of sexual love," Nietzsche wrote, "has been glorified and deified so much in all ages—indeed . . . this love has furnished the concept of love as the opposite of egoism while it actually may be the most ingenuous expression of egoism."

Nietzsche also perceived the antagonistic paradoxes of sex and birth as experienced in women's bodies, how birth positioned them somewhere between gods and beasts. Expected to be chaste and ignorant until marriage, marriage hurled them suddenly "as by a gruesome lightning bolt, into reality and knowledge." Through sex, women "catch love and shame in a contradiction," Nietzsche believed, and are "forced to experience at the same time delight, surrender, duty, pity, terror." This results in what he called a "psychic knot" like no other, a knot within which birth, too, is tied. A woman can only respond to this hard knot with silence, he argued. Her eyes close even on herself. What except silence and blindness are adequate responses to such an enigmatic riddle?

As Nietzsche was prying into women's psychic silences, more and more women were writing about experiences that had largely been unspeakable: sex, desire, birth, love, and motherhood, as experienced by women. They didn't need a man like Nietzsche to depict birth or female sexuality for them; they had pen and paper and could do that themselves. Their depictions, however, and women's depictions of birth down to this day, resonate curiously with Nietzsche's. Birth can be a profoundly destabilizing experience, chaotic and anarchic, but it can also be ecstatic, transformative, and even liberating, a restructuring of the human/self/other/divine order. As Louise Erdrich wrote of her pregnancy in the late twentieth century, "I fear I've made a ship inside a bottle. I'll have to break." There's the birth, the breaking, and then, she reports, "the mystery of an epiphany, the sense of oceanic oneness, the great yes, the wholeness." How supremely Nietzschean she sounds.

As more women started writing, they narrated birth's profoundly liberatory and creative potential, but also its destructiveness and even its horrors. In their complexity, their stories offer cautionary tales about any easy, uncomplicated, and immaculate account of birth and new beginnings. Before returning to the twentieth century and the women who wrote about childbirth alongside Arendt and after her, I need to first spool backward, back to the turn of the eighteenth century, when God's authority was being eroded, humans were assuming godlike, creative roles on the world's stages, and women were starting to write about their experiences with pregnancy, labor, and birth with greater frequency, as they tried to imagine a more active role in their own societies and to discover within birth the framework for their liberation.

The Soul Most Alive to Tenderness

Mary Wollstonecraft was born in London on April 27, 1759. The second child and oldest daughter in a family that would eventually include seven children, she would go on to become a leading voice of the Age of Enlightenment and a radical forerunner of the modern feminist movement. Her life would be tragically cut short, however, when she died giving birth to her second daughter at the age of thirty-eight. In her life, she witnessed how birth endangered and challenged women and children, but she also recognized birth's importance for any society. She saw in birth a creative, embodied, nurturing richness and intimacy, out of which society could reimagine itself to create a more just and equal human order. She was ahead of her time in understanding the role of natal nurture in both individual lives and in the lives of communities. Ultimately taken down by birth, she left a body of written work shot through with the spirit of natality, a work infused with a "resistless energy" and expressive of a "soul . . . most alive to tenderness."

Wollstonecraft's politically oriented version of natality has challenged readers for centuries with its insistence on equality for the sexes, its sensitivity to the lives of women, children, and the poor, its immersion in the natural world, and its commitment to a life shared with other people. She wrote passionately in letters, declarations, articles, and novels, imagining a more just human order and drafting what her biographer Lyndall Gordon calls "a blueprint for human change." She would be "the first of a new genus," she proclaimed to her sister.

Upon her birth, however, she was merely a first daughter for her family. Immediately after her birth, her mother packed her off to a wet nurse; she would only rejoin the family after her first year. One of the most pronounced critiques Wollstonecraft would make in what became her most famous work was her excoriation of mothers who don't nurse their own children, relegating that task to subservient women. Infant formula, of course, was not available in the eighteenth century. If you wanted your baby to live, you either nursed it yourself or had someone else do it for you.

As Wollstonecraft remembered her, her mother was overwhelmed and neglectful, submissive and cold, preferring her older brother to Mary and her younger siblings. From a young age, she was charged with heavy domestic and childcare duties as her mother languished with various ailments. Her father, meanwhile, was a hot-blooded, violent alcoholic plagued by a dangerous mix of class grievance and entitlement, who would set his family on a path of dramatic downward mobility, squandering his sizable inheritance and leaving his children destitute. Wollstonecraft grew up hearing her father rape her mother at night; she listened to her mother's screams through the thin walls of their various homes. As a teenager, she grew defiant. She'd set up guard outside her mother's bedroom door in an attempt to shield her from her father's violent rage when he returned home late at night. It wasn't, to say the least, a happy home.

Wollstonecraft saw in her parents' marriage a mirror of the tyranny in the political and economic world all around her, in an industrializing England where class divisions rankled, women's status was worsening, child labor powered factories, and slavery was still legal. In eighteenth-century England, women had considerably fewer legal rights than they had had before the Norman Conquest, seven centuries earlier. A wife and her children were considered a husband's property, and she had no right to a divorce. A man was legally allowed to beat his wife or starve her. He could deny her medical care, confine her to the home, or send her off to an asylum with the simple attestation that she'd gone crazy. If she left him, she had no right to the children she had gestated and borne out of her own body. Statesman and philosopher Edmund Burke, who was old enough to be Wollstonecraft's father, praised the patriarchal family as the "little platoon" that we must learn to love. But Wollstonecraft wanted to free the family from such weaponized, violent metaphors and to reimagine the domestic realm in more tender and egalitarian terms.

She was living in a time of rapid epistemic change, of paradigmatic political and social revolution that was accompanied by seismic shifts in religious belief following the Scientific Revolution and the industrializing century that had preceded it. In European salons, cafés, and publications, intellectuals espoused ideas about reason, equality, liberty, and progress that would result in the late eighteenth-century revolutions in America, France, and Haiti which overthrew monarchical regimes and attempted to found democratic societies. Wollstonecraft was a teenager when the American Revolution began, and she was introduced to revolutionary, liberal philosophers like John Locke.

Over a century later, imagining a creative lineage linking herself to this trailblazing woman, Virginia Woolf argued that the eighteenth century's political revolutions were not just Wollstonecraft's backdrop. Revolution was instead "an active agent in her own blood," and in her, human nature was being constantly reborn.

o o o

At the age of nineteen, Wollstonecraft left her unhappy home and went out into the world, attempting to survive by her wits and make enough money to support herself. It was a rare and bold move for a woman of her class and time to make. But she never cut ties with her family. She nursed her mother through a sickness until her death in 1782, and she provided for her sisters when her father quickly remarried their housekeeper and moved away.

Her mother's death and her father's abandonment left the daughters with few options other than to hawk themselves desperately on the marriage market, no easy task as they had no dowries. One of her younger sisters, Bess, was married off quickly. Her brother made the arrangements, hoping for the best for his sister, but Wollstonecraft was less optimistic about Bess's prospects. In a letter she expressed her distrust of marriage, vowing, "I will not marry, for I don't want to be tied to this nasty world." This theme of being tied to the world would repeat itself in her work, but she would eventually see those ties more positively.

One month into the marriage, Bess was pregnant, and after a difficult labor, she gave birth to a little girl she named Mary after her sister. She seems to have loved the child, but the birth sent her into "fits of phrensy." Bess's mental state rapidly deteriorated, and Wollstonecraft was eventually summoned. Upon arrival, she gathered her sister in her arms, trying to soothe her. But Bess was inconsolable and discombobulated; something had gone terribly wrong in the marriage and she felt ill-used. Had she been raped like her mother, or was her husband just oblivious to her needs? Or maybe birth had initiated the phrensy, and this was a case of post-natal depression or even post-natal psychosis. Either way, Bess could be locked up by her husband and declared a madwoman. As she had no right to divorce, the sisters devised an escape plan, one that sadly involved leaving Bess's newborn baby behind, as she possessed no legal right to her child.

Wollstonecraft despaired over the vulnerability she witnessed in her childbearing sister and the daughter she gave birth to. She had ample cause for concern. Her niece died before her first birthday. The following year, in 1785, Mary traveled all the way to Lisbon on a sailboat to help her beloved childhood friend Fanny Blood, who had become pregnant with her first child also after only a month of marriage, and who confessed to her friend that she was extremely depressed. Fanny's health had never been strong, and Wollstonecraft knew the dangers childbirth held for her.

On a windy Monday in November of 1785, Fanny gave birth to a baby boy mere hours after Wollstonecraft arrived from England, but the happy event quickly turned into a nightmare. The baby was underweight and Fanny's own health was rapidly failing. "I am now beginning to awake out of a terrifying dream," Wollstonecraft wrote to her sisters. "Fanny is so worn out her recovery would be almost a resurrection." She tried to resign herself to the likelihood of her best friend's death, but she couldn't help clinging to the faint hope that Fanny would live. She hired a wet nurse and prayed by Fanny's bedside for her miraculous return to health, but within a week, her beloved friend had died. Wollstonecraft cared for the orphaned baby for weeks but finally had to return to England. After her departure, Fanny's baby son followed his mother into the grave.

Heartbroken over these deathly births, Wollstonecraft listened closely to a reverend's instruction: "*study* the scenes of sorrow," learn from these losses, do not forget the shades of death that have gathered around you. "Keep thy heart with all diligence," he advised her, quoting Proverbs, "for out of it are the issues of life." She responded by plunging back into life, seeking its next scenes, channeling her creative energies into writing, where she could productively vent her frustrations about the challenges women faced.

o o o

Out in the world on her own, while still playing mother to her sisters, Wollstonecraft worked as a teacher, a governess, a translator, and a reviewer, and she published her first novel and works of criticism before writing, over the course of an impassioned six weeks, the work she'd become most known for: *A Vindication of the Rights of Woman*. This bracing manifesto was published in 1792, seven years after Fanny's death. In it, she critiqued her misogynist culture and imagined a different, utopian social and moral future for humanity, one in which women's liberation was not separate from other liberatory movements, from the abolition of slavery to participatory democracy. *Vindication* caused a little uproar in its day, prompting calls to burn Wollstonecraft in effigy, but today it reads as both revolutionary and conservative, surprisingly dissonant with the more individualistic, secular version of liberalism that capitalism helped nurture. Wollstonecraft imagined a human individual whose rights and freedoms were integrated into a community's ethics of care and were balanced with interpersonal duties.

It's an angry book, one that "loudly demands JUSTICE" for women, but it's also an optimistic, sensitive, and large-hearted one, a book inspired by an "affection for the whole human race" and written with the conviction that there's a truth common to us all, a democratic commonness violated by all forms of slavery and domination. To see it, we just need to root ourselves perseveringly and pantingly in the thick of human experience. The revolution she imagined was a moral one; words like virtue, modesty, duty, sincerity, affection, gentleness, and nursing cascade through the pages of *Vindication*, supporting her ideas about reason and political change, rather than obstructing them. To take care of themselves and their families, women need to understand their bodies. Children should be taught where babies come from. Why, she asks, are children not told that their mothers carried them and gestated them in the way a mother cat does her kittens? Children can wrap their nascent minds around such basic, bodily facts.

Wollstonecraft was a critic of marriage, but she believed in the importance of family. A father should not be out "visiting the harlot" and a mother should not be consumed by "the arts of coquetry." Rather, they should both be focused on nurturing, protecting, and educating their children. If a man does not take seriously his responsibilities as a father, a woman will never get over her coquettish ambitions to keep her husband's attention exclusively on her, to wield over him the little power she has. Women's emancipation and the attendant revolution of social mores Wollstonecraft envisioned weren't about women gaining the freedom to deny their domestic, familial, maternal duties and to prance out into the world as coquettes or libertines, as vain, preening adornments to the present order. Emancipation meant that they would gain the freedoms and ethos necessary to perform their interpersonal duties with steadfastness, strength, and persevering energy, to care for the people around them and to raise a next generation that had learned the tenderness of deep, selfless affections.

She saw a real problem in the "artificial weakness" the women

of her age, class, and race were encouraged to feign, in obsequious-
ness to the gender hierarchy. Women *were* strong, and they needed
to *act* strong. The problem was not just that pretending to be weak
obscured women's natural vigor; it also fostered "a propensity to
tyrannize, and gives birth to cunning, the natural opponent of
strength." Ideas about women's ladylike fragility—especially and
ironically the weakness of the more powerful classes—provided the
context and rationale for the exploitation of other classes and races of
people, particularly in the transatlantic slave trade. The female slave
was treated as an inexhaustible, energetic laborer whose servile body
experienced few limits, subservient to but always physically stronger
than her mistress. Women's oppression, their weakness, had paradoxically bred in them the potential for despotism. The oppressed
could become the oppressor, Wollstonecraft believed. And humans
were not born to master and tyrannize other human beings, but to
nurture them. She imagined a more democratic order in which the
work associated with the body wasn't relegated to certain groups of
unpaid people—women and slaves.

Wollstonecraft lived during an era of imperial expansion and
the height of the slave trade—a trade both contradicted by Enlightenment ideas about equality and supported by notions of human
agency, knowledge, exploration, and progress. She understood well
that one group of people becoming free at the expense of another
group was a despotic freedom at best. And she was suspicious of
ideas about human mastery, of a freedom without bodily, interpersonal, and even spiritual limits.

Wollstonecraft believed that humankind's emancipation could
run into problems if it entailed a rebellion against not just human,
religious, and political authority, but also against nature and God
himself. *Vindication* expresses Wollstonecraft's belief in God as the

creator of all human life. "I build my belief," she wrote, "on the per-
fection of God." The knot that ties us to a providential source, like
our ties to one another, is not easy to untie. "Could the helpless creature whom he called from nothing," she asked, "break loose from
his providence, and boldly learn to know good by practising evil
without his permission?" A generation later, haunted by her death,
Wollstonecraft's daughter Mary Godwin Shelley would be left asking the same question as she wrote through the sadness and chaos of
childbirth and infancy's devastations.

o o o

The year that *Vindication* was published, Wollstonecraft traveled to
France to report on the French Revolution, a revolution in which she
saw the promise of a new, emancipatory era. But once in Paris, she
observed with increasing horror the devastation of the city and the
bloodthirsty excesses of the Reign of Terror. Amid her increasing
disillusion, however, she experienced a liberatory atmosphere and
a sociability that she felt had been denied her back in England. She
became romantically interested in men; passionate, amorous emotions arose in her. Even as she was advocating for women's independence, she fell in love with an American speculator, Captain Gilbert
Imlay, a witty, handsome ladies' man who was attracted by Wollstonecraft's intelligence and who shared her belief in liberty and the
equality of women. Perhaps they could pioneer a new relationship
between the sexes, Wollstonecraft thought, and could experience a
passionate equality freed of any institutionalized imprimatur. She
went to his apartment and had sex for the first time, swept into a
reverie of romantic exuberance and sexual fulfillment.

They didn't marry but they moved in together and soon there-
after, Wollstonecraft was pregnant. She was excited to be pregnant,
but also troubled by what she started to experience around this time:

how Imlay's money-making ventures drew him away from home and from her for long stretches. She felt neglected and grew depressed as he built his fortune, but she was romantically renewed by his attention when he returned. Through the seesaw of her emotional pregnancy, she kept writing, imagining forms of government based on the protection of the weak. "Liberty with maternal wing," she wrote, "seems to be soaring to regions far above vulgar annoyance, promising to shelter all mankind." The governments of the future would be more like mothers, she prophesied, caring lovingly for their children. The political realm and the domestic realm were connected, an idea which would percolate through twentieth-century feminism.

In the spring of 1794, at the age of thirty-five, with the French Revolution and a bloody guillotine as her immediate backdrop, she gave birth at home with the assistance of one midwife to her first daughter, Fanny, named after her childhood friend who had died in childbirth. She and her "vigorous little Girl" thrived in the immediate postnatal period. "Nothing," she boasted in a letter written six days after the delivery, "could be more natural or easy than my labour." "I feel great pleasure," she wrote, "at being a mother." She reveled in the pleasures of new motherhood, nursing her baby as she hadn't been nursed as an infant, and celebrating her own natural, birthing strength. She and Fanny didn't "lie in" or stay inside through the postnatal period, as was the custom at the time. Wollstonecraft returned quickly to the world, toting Fanny along with her everywhere she went.

o o o

As Bess Wollstonecraft and Fanny Blood's stories make clear, not all babies and mothers had such an easy time in childbirth during the eighteenth century. It was an age of great scientific advances, but these advances resulted in setbacks when it came to childbirth and women's bodies. Medical and anatomical knowledge grew greatly in this period, and obstetrics was founded as a branch of medicine. Male doctors became routinely involved in childbirth for the first time in history, a development with disastrous consequences. From the seventeenth century onward, hospitals began replacing the home as the site in which many women—especially, initially, poor women—gave birth, with doctors performing the role that female midwives had filled in most societies since the beginnings of recorded history. Science superseded the womanly art and magic—the witchery, even—of midwifery. Called lying-in hospitals, these public, doctor-run wards were dangerous, crowded, contaminated places for birthing women.

The scientific community had not yet made the connection between bacteria and the infections they caused, and so unsuspecting doctors were routinely infecting the patients whose health they believed themselves to be maintaining. Doctors and students went from woman to woman in these crowded wards, not washing their hands or changing their clothes, using the same tools from delivery to delivery. It wasn't unusual for doctors to move straight from corpses in a morgue to the delivery table, bringing bacteria from decomposing bodies directly to the bodies of women in labor. Puerperal fever, which usually developed in the uterine tract, came to a woman shortly after she gave birth, and it was seen as mysterious. Autopsies performed after maternal deaths revealed "thick fetid pus suffocating the ovaries, uterus, and abdomen. New mothers rotted away." Breast milk, anxiety, constipation, and cold air were all suspected as the cause, and feverish mothers were treated with toxins, emetics, quinine, douches, and leeches. In the eighteenth century, puerperal fever was the leading cause of maternal mortality and, after tuberculosis, the greatest threat to women of childbearing age.

The practice of packing newborns off to wet nurses also had negative consequences. During that era in Paris, only about a third of mothers nursed their own children. The practice had fallen out of fashion. Nursing and sex were seen as incompatible, and after birth a husband's needs took precedence over a baby's needs. Wollstonecraft was trying to imagine a culture in which a child wouldn't be sacrificed at birth to its father's lusty needs. The question was urgent; half of French babies died in a wet nurse's care. In the wet nurses' crowded cottages, babies were hung from beams in harnesses, with little chance to move and with rags stuffed in their mouths to mute their wailing. Wollstonecraft was sure that the effect of that postnatal estrangement from a mother who might more lovingly care for her baby was significant.

The practice had great costs for wet nurses and their families as well. Although wet-nursing provided relatively highly paid work to poor and working-class women who otherwise had limited opportunities, the practice was based on an unethical foundation. Women whose bodies were producing milk were new mothers themselves, and they were enlisted into physically taxing labor in a state of physical vulnerability. Wet nurses did this work because they were in economically or socially precarious conditions. As a cottage industry, it drew in illegitimate mothers who had given up their own children, or poor women who had to deny their own child milk in order to feed it to the babies of well-paying strangers. In her book on the history of infant feeding, Valerie Fildes concludes that "in effect, wealthy parents frequently 'bought' the life of their infant for the life of another."

Wollstonecraft's insistence on using a midwife rather than a doctor and on nursing her own child may have saved her life, her child's life, and the life of a child born to some wet-nursing woman.

o o o

Wollstonecraft took to motherhood, but Imlay quickly lost interest in family life. Her letters to him became more desperate and accusatory. She pleaded with him to return but he increasingly stayed away, leaving her to her own devices as a single, unwed mother with a newborn child. She was devastated; in addition to the social and economic precariousness she experienced as an unwed mother, and the physical demands of pregnancy, birth, and the postnatal period, she also understood that she had acquiesced to a state of dependence she had never imagined herself capable of, thirsting for the adoration of a man.

In 1795, a year after giving birth, outcast by her society, alone, and struggling to take care of a child while continuing to write, she grew abysmally depressed. She attempted suicide, overdosing on laudanum, which failed to kill her. Trying to begin again, she traveled to Scandinavia on some business of Imlay's and wrote there her commercially and critically successful book *Letters Written in Sweden, Norway, and Denmark*. Comprised of a series of letters, the book reads like a travelogue, and it ranges from the personal to the political, from melancholy depths to sublime heights. Fanny had traveled to Scandinavia with her, and she makes appearances in the book. Wollstonecraft describes observing her child so calmly sleeping, and of feeling emotions that "trembled on the brink of extacy and agony . . . which made me feel more alive than usual." She was no "particle broken off from the grand mass of mankind," she realized in gazing at her daughter. She was instead part of a "mighty whole." "Futurity," she continued, "what hast thou not to give to those who know that there is such a thing as happiness!"

The book is filled with delicious details: comfortable beds, shining pewter on shelves, a silver crescent of moon, luxurious rest, and melodious winds whispering through open windows. "Paradise," she wrote, "was before me. My little cherub was again hiding her face in my bosom. I heard her sweet cooing beat on my heart from the cliffs, and saw her tiny footsteps on the sands. New-born hopes seemed, like the rainbow, to appear in the clouds of sorrow, faint, yet sufficient to amuse away despair." A buoyant natality charges such passages, but elsewhere in the book, her sense of natality is more foreboding. Catching sight of some soldiers, "beings training to be sold to slaughter, or be slaughtered," she suddenly despairs over creation's design. The Deity who controls nature seems invested in the human species but not in the lives of individuals. "Blossoms come forth only to be blighted," she laments, and "fish lay their spawn where it will be devoured; and what a large portion of the human race are born merely to be swept prematurely away." She continues, "Children peep into existence, suffer, and die; men play like moths about a candle, and sink into the flame; war, and 'the thousand ills which flesh is heir to,' mow them down in shoals, whilst the more cruel prejudices of society palsies existence, introducing not less sure, though slower decay."

She returned from her three-month journey through Scandinavia to London only to discover to her horror that Imlay was living with an actress. She attempted suicide again, trying to drown herself in the Thames. She nearly succeeded, but a boatman found her body floating unconscious and he dragged her back to a tavern where a stranger resuscitated her. She blamed the suicide attempts on Imlay's poor treatment of her, but it's hard to not imagine birth's role in her distress, given how much more we know now about postnatal depression and the arduous physical and psychic demands of new motherhood. Wollstonecraft existed for some months "in a living tomb" and her life became an "exercise of fortitude, continually on the stretch." She was "unwilling to cut the Gordian knot" that bound her to Imlay, but a break would come, facilitating a rebirth aided by spending time in nature.

She recovered by giving up on the prospect of a life with Imlay but also by coming to the slow understanding that she, as a person passionately dedicated to other people, occupied a higher moral ground than he did, in all his aloof, moneymaking liberty. She came to see that her passionate commitment to him and to her child was not a violation of her ideas about female emancipation; they were simply the painfully lived, experiential realization of what she'd argued all along: that we are ardently bound to other people, that it is a sign of perfect reason to take affectionate care of the people we are responsible for.

When her younger sister Bess married, she had written that "I will not marry, for I don't want to be tied to this nasty world." But she was beginning to appreciate how there really wasn't an alternative to being tied to this nasty world. The world might be nasty, but it's where we're born and where we'll live out our days. We cannot untie ourselves from this difficult world, as we have no other world to claim. As she matured personally and intellectually, she articulated a creed that, Virginia Woolf believed, was "fitted to meet the sordid misery of real human life."

"Every day she made theories," Woolf wrote, "by which life should be lived; and every day she came smack against the rock of other people's prejudices." She was neither a pedant nor a "cold-blooded theorist"—for "something was born in her that thrust aside her theories and forced her to model them afresh." Woolf believed that Wollstonecraft's conflicts and contradictions exhibited themselves on her face, a face "at once so resolute and so dreamy, so sensual and so intelligent, and beautiful into the bargain with its great coils of hair and the large bright eyes."

She was recovering from the heartbreak of her abandonment and the trauma of her suicide attempts when she became reacquainted with William Godwin, the son of a minister and a celebrated radical philosopher. He believed in mind above matter, in a mental perfectibility that would enable people to avoid sickness and aging and to become immortal, in a rationalism stripped of both pleasures and pain. He has been associated with utilitarianism, with rationalist ideas about the consequences of actions. In one famous case, he asked whom one should save from a burning room: Archbishop Fénelon, who was about to write his consequential *Télémaque*, or a pregnant chambermaid who might become the reader's mother (or wife). If, for instance, Fénelon would have a more significant positive impact on the world than you would, then you should leave that mere chambermaid, your future mother, to burn to her death—and obviate your own existence in the bargain.

Godwin was also, as far as is known, a virgin when he and Wollstonecraft met this time, although he had gathered around him a flock of female admirers vying for his attention. For all his rebellious ideas, he was stiff and ministerial, austere and wedded strictly to routines. This "little man with the big head" had dined with Wollstonecraft years before her romance with Imlay and had been put off by how she had dominated the conversation. He had also found her *Vindication* messy. But when they ran into each other again in January of 1796, he discovered her softened by her sorrows, more sympathetic and more available. He was struck by her "newborn peace." Their intimacy grew as he edited her manuscript of a play based on her relationship with Imlay. He condescendingly considered it crude and he criticized her careless grammar and syntax, but she took this in stride, perhaps because she was simply so used to criticism by this point. Or perhaps she was just terribly lonely, grateful for any attentive energies directed at her and her creative work from a man she admired. Either way, the relationship grew more affectionate, in the shared space of their radicalism and the written word. They became lovers that summer and Wollstonecraft again conceived.

o o o

Both Wollstonecraft and Godwin had been vocal critics of marriage, seeing in it all the tyranny they hated, but her pregnancy made them change their minds. Godwin understood the trials Wollstonecraft faced as an unmarried mother, and he wanted to shield her and his child from public censure. In his mind, he wasn't a hypocrite; he could marry the woman he loved and still abhor marriage as an institution. Besides, their marriage wouldn't be conventional. They would both continue with their writing, and they would keep separate quarters. Why, furthermore, should they be strictly bound by any theory?

They married quietly in an old country church several months into Wollstonecraft's pregnancy and settled into a happy life of domesticity. His wife was, Godwin proclaimed, a "worshipper of domestic life." Pregnancy for her was a mark of her inequality as decreed by nature, but it was also, paradoxically, "the source of a thousand endearments." New feelings were "coming to birth in her," Virginia Woolf wrote, looking back at Wollstonecraft's pregnancy about 130 years later, and her relationship with Godwin would be her "most fruitful experiment."

In June of 1797, Wollstonecraft was six months pregnant and Godwin was away. They wrote each other affectionate letters. Godwin asked how she was feeling, and how Fanny was doing. Still scarred by Imlay's abandonment, Wollstonecraft was touched by Godwin's attentiveness to her and to her young child. She wrote promptly and warmly in response, describing how her unborn child frisked joyfully inside her, creating disturbances she didn't appear to mind. "I begin to love this little creature, and to anticipate his birth as a fresh twist to a knot, which I do not wish to untie," she wrote. Not holding anything back, she gushed to Godwin, "I love you better than I supposed I did, when I promised to love you for ever . . . You are a tender, affectionate creature; and I feel it thrilling through my frame giving and promising pleasure."

Nietzsche, again, identified a tightly tied psychic knot at the heart of women's experience, how in marriage they caught love and shame in a contradiction, with the chaste bride experiencing sex like a "gruesome lightning bolt" on her wedding night. Silence, he believed, was how women responded to the unresolvable contradictions unique to their gender. Women kept mum and, in apparent shame and confusion, they closed their eyes on their own experience.

But maybe muteness wasn't the only response to this difficult tangle. Maybe women didn't need to look away from themselves and from the problems in their lives. Wollstonecraft was not staying silent or closing her eyes. To begin with, she hadn't been the chaste bride, arriving blushing and bashful at the marital bed. She was already the mother of one child, and sex wasn't a gruesome lightning bolt; she appears to have enjoyed it.

For Wollstonecraft, the body was not a problem to be solved, although she was swimming against certain philosophic tides. Mind and soul are entirely different from the body, mind–body dualist René Descartes had argued in the century before Wollstonecraft was born. He had boasted that he could imagine having no body, as if thinking of the body's experiences, or deriving intellectual, aesthetic, or spiritual significance from them, would be to cross over some inviolable line in the sand of consciousness. But the body—its natality and mortality, its weaknesses, pleasures, and needs—could not be eradicated by any idea, Mary Wollstonecraft could see, a point hammered in by her experiences of sex, pregnancy, and childbirth.

As her daughter gestated in her body, Wollstonecraft was trying to think and to write. She began work on a series of "Letters on the Management of Infants" and on instruction books for children, neither of which came to fruition. Fatigue, childcare, and various domestic duties distracted Wollstonecraft from her creative work during the pregnancy, but she still somehow wrote and published an article for a new radical journal. "On Poetry, and Our Relish for the Beauties of Nature" is a short, lyrical essay that expresses a nascent Romanticism and defends the poetic writing style she had long been cultivating. This is, I'd argue, a natal style. The essay is infused with natality; it's buoyed by her blossoming love, her natal physicality and hope, her gestational sense of the natural world, and her continuing recognition of a sublime divinity. The essay would, within months, become clouded by the tragic shadow of her untimely death. But on the page, it has stayed alive and inexhaustible, wedged spontaneously and perilously between the fullness of newly gestating life and the sudden finality of death.

The essay starts with the primacy of observation, with the importance of seeing the world through our own eyes and perceiving it through our senses, rather than relying on bookish knowledge or any lessons learned secondhand. Like Hannah Arendt, Wollstonecraft sought that direct line between thought and experience. She observes the dew, the grass, and the sun rising in "solitary majesty" with its "beautifying beams." In their immediacy and in "all their native wildness," these natural details invigorate our minds and enliven our enthusiasms. They make us more alive. Like Friedrich Nietzsche returning from his lonely walks, she describes "the richness of the soil," and imagines a poetic sensibility born where the Apollonian and Dionysian meet at their fertilization point and the world becomes pregnant with a "resistless energy." This meeting point is where the "soul was most alive to tenderness." Like both Arendt and Nietzsche, Wollstonecraft reaches back toward the "poetry written in the infancy of society," to find a style infused with nature's power. For the ancients, a deity was nearby, present in all the clouds, and he walked on the waves. The divine mind that formed the world bled into the human mind that contemplated it; there was no estrangement, no painful separation. Creator, creation, and the creative artist merged.

Like Nietzsche, Wollstonecraft critiques advanced civilizations, for the ways in which their people have grown away from their primal, natural source, and for how their creative artists have become mere artificial imitators, rather than active participants in nature. A work that stays close to its source is messier, less voluntary, less polished, and less subject to editing or analysis than the "advanced" civilization's soberer—and ultimately barren—artworks. These were the kinds of insults that had been hurled at her own work, even by her husband: that it was messy. But maybe humans *are* messy. She argued for rawness as an aesthetic attribute, opening up room for a person like her, a woman lacking an elite education, to be the producer of a great work of art. "The silken wings of fancy," she wrote, "are shrivelled by rules; and a desire of attaining elegance of diction, occasions an attention to words, incompatible with sublime, impassioned thoughts." She imagined a poetic idiom that seeks the chaotic, carnal, physical substance rather than the shadows, seeking a relaxation into the material world that leads one into the "voluptuary."

In the last paragraph of this essay, perhaps remembering the tumult of her failed romance and single motherhood, she strikes a note of caution, warning that this same sublimated sensibility, based on a quickness of the senses, can lead one merely to libertinism. What should be preferred is more moderate and modest: a virtuous life of affection and friendship. Perhaps she had in mind the other book she was writing at this time, one that never got finished: *The Wrongs of Women*, a gritty, dark novel about female sexual exploitation and oppression. Women's inequality and the violence they suffered remained her concerns. At the same time, she was buoyed by natal hopes. She wrote to Godwin about not wishing to untie the knot of her pregnancy. Godwin responded with effusive affection, noting how they were (in gestating a new being) multiplying their consciousnesses, even "at the hazard . . . of opening new avenues for pain and misery to attack us."

o o o

On August 30, 1797, Wollstonecraft woke with contractions. She summoned a midwife and prepared for what she thought would be a quick labor, like the labor she'd experienced with her first child. But her second child did not come so easily. She paced and read and wrote notes to her husband, who was holed up in his office. Finally, close to midnight, a baby girl was born and they named her Mary Wollstonecraft Godwin. The baby was pale, weak, and underweight, but they were overjoyed, basking in the new life they held in their hands, the unification of their souls.

But there was a problem: the placenta had not come out after the baby was delivered, and this put Wollstonecraft at risk of developing the uterine infection to which so many women succumbed. Wollstonecraft believed she and the midwife could take care of the situation, but Godwin insisted on calling a doctor from the hospital. The doctor arrived before dawn and proceeded to tear out the placenta in pieces, without offering any anesthetic. Wollstonecraft lost a massive amount of blood, and she confessed to her husband that she had never known such bodily pain. She experienced a series of fainting fits and thought she would die. The doctor left, believing no doubt that he had saved her life. Wollstonecraft smiled at her husband and told him she was determined to live.

After a few days, however, Wollstonecraft spiked a fever, which caused her to shake so violently that her bed banged loudly against the wall as her teeth chattered. A different doctor came and gave his diagnosis: puerperal fever. Pieces of the placenta were still stuck in Wollstonecraft's womb, and the rot had set in. There was nothing he could do to save her, although a series of doctors came in and out, inspecting her and confirming that she was doomed. For a week or so, she slipped in and out of consciousness and shivered with sepsis. Her breasts hardened so dangerously with contaminated milk that puppies were brought in to suckle her. Her mind devolved into "too decayed a state," until finally, on September 10, she died, with Godwin close beside her. He was shocked that the body he had known as so animate, so alive with passionate intensity, was now so entirely lifeless. And there he was: a radical who was now also a single father of two young daughters, one of whom was a sickly newborn who needed the nursing and affection her mother had so deeply believed was essential.

The baby, Mary Wollstonecraft Godwin, who later became Mary Godwin Shelley, would grow up motherless, give birth five times herself, and outlive many of her own babies. She would follow in her mother's footsteps as a writer and would author one of the greatest birth stories ever written: the gothic nineteenth-century novel *Frankenstein*. As a newborn, she was left to her bereaved father's care. Her motherlessness and her mother's sacrificial death were shared by some of the other leading English women writers of the next century: Emily and Charlotte Brontë, George Eliot, and Virginia Woolf all also lost their mothers in childbirth, and those deaths hung over women's emerging literary tradition.

Mary Shelley never got over the loss of her mother. It haunted her life and her work and foreshadowed some of the different losses she would experience as a birthing mother. She carried forth Wollstonecraft's unfinished projects and convictions, exploring new dimensions of creativity and birth, asking new questions about the relationship between art, birth, and a creator God whom many nineteenth-century intellectuals believed was ceding his creative powers to them: to rational, scientific human producers who generated, created, proliferated, and controlled realities that they laid claim to like fathers, asserting their authority and their legal ownership. Mary Shelley imagined a darker version of natality than Wollstonecraft's, more doubting of the powers of human generativity, less convinced of the positive role of human reason in any scheme of creation, and less believing in the benevolence of either God or nature.

For all her depressive episodes, Mary Wollstonecraft was a lover of life in all its various forms. She was an advocate for the unborn, the born, and the dying alike and was even a defender of animals, recognizing the sanctity of nonhuman life forms. The painfulness of reading her, so alive and so disarmingly passionate on the page, lies not just in witnessing the struggles she experienced as the daughter of an abusive father, as a single working mother and a jilted lover, or as a vilified pioneer in the struggle for women's emancipation, but in all the thrills and pains and pleasures she never got to experience. She was among natality's most ardent disciples, and she died too young. Virginia Woolf described the "high-handed and hot-blooded" way in which Wollstonecraft "cut her way to the quick of life." "She is alive and active," Woolf wrote, and "we hear her voice and trace her influence even now among the living."

The Workshop of Filthy Creation

"We think back through our mothers if we are women," wrote Virginia Woolf in her classic book *A Room of One's Own*. She had just observed how much discouragement and criticism various nineteenth-century women novelists endured as they created their art. But this scorn and rejection paled in comparison with the greater challenge they faced: the lack of a tradition behind them, the "scarcity and inadequacy of tools." When they turned to the literary tradition their cultures had nurtured, they found sentences and shapes—narrative arcs and literary domes—that were written by men and that were alien to their own lived experience. They could not think back through texts, through the written word. Their thinking was anchored instead in a bodily ancestry, one that had largely not been written down. A book, Woolf believed, must be "adapted to the body."

Woolf imagined books focused on thematic concerns different from those written by men, and also alive with different rhythms, full of interruptions, fluctuating between work and rest, animated by twists and turns, concentrated and yet soft in their shapes. In Woolf's account, a novel is an alive medium, animated like a body— a body not exclusively male or female but, rather, expressive of the fertilization point between the genders. Such a work could express the "vastness and variety of the world," not merely one aspect of it. Men can also think back through their mothers and can thereby access a new, natal sensibility.

But in the nineteenth century, most male writers were not particularly natally oriented. When they depicted women's bodies, they didn't emphasize their natality; they stressed their mortality. Dead, dying, and sickly women were immortalized in the works of male writers in the Victorian era, a period in which rapid industrialization had deepened the divisions between the genders in England, resulting in more distinct spheres of home and work—cutting off the private, maternal realm from the public world, where men as active citizens were shaping culture, industry, and politics. Women like Mary Wollstonecraft had forged a difficult path into literary and political communities, emphasizing women's strength and vitality; but in the next generation, women of her class, race, and nationality were becoming saintly icons of domesticity, weakness, and mortality. In 1846, Edgar Allan Poe described the death of a beautiful woman as "unquestionably the most poetic topic in the world."

If the death of a beautiful woman was poetic, what would Poe and his male peers have made of Mary Wollstonecraft's death? The literary tradition had little place for such a woman and such a death. Wollstonecraft, well into her pregnancy with Mary Shelley, had defined the poetic as a style unmediated by books, by a literary tradition largely authored by men, one building toward these dead, beautiful, poetic women of the Victorian era. The pregnancy she was experiencing was only represented in that tradition secondhand, from an observing distance and filtered through the lens of a classical education to which most women still did not have access. She was trying to give birth to a new sensibility, to imagine a literary aesthetic that was based on immediate sensations, to create a body of work that was the product of a strong and active mind directly observing and responding to her world. She would deliver Mary Wollstonecraft Godwin (here called Mary Shelley or simply Mary) into life, but that life was conditioned by mortality as much as by natality. After birth, her newborn daughter would miss that poetic experience of the immediate sensations of her mother's body in its active, alive, and natal wildness. She would grow up in the shadow of her mother's fatality, living in her mother's presence, but with that presence mediated by art and the written word.

A portrait of Mary Wollstonecraft hung in the house she grew up in, looking down upon her as she went about her days. Her mother was also kept alive in the books she had written. Mary Shelley, bookish from an early age, would be a lifelong reader of her mother's work, drawing inspiration and solace from her mother's example. She was her mother's most devoted disciple, but her mother existed only in the ransacked realm of memory that Wollstonecraft had been wary of. "The memory of my mother," Mary Shelley wrote, "has always been the pride and delight of my life."

o o o

Mary Shelley was born as the English summer wound to its close, on August 30, 1797. Her mother was dead ten days later. William Godwin responded to his wife's death by retreating forlornly into his study, leaving Mary and her sister in the care of a housekeeper. Grieving, he quickly composed *Memoirs of the Author of the Rights of Woman*. First published in January of 1798, Godwin's book was an honest attempt to capture the remarkable and unconventional life of a woman he loved. It was also, some have felt, his attempt to control the narrative, to author the life of a woman he had only known for two of her eventful thirty-eight years.

His authorship of her life was consequential. The publication of *Memoirs* celebrated his wife's unconventional life but, in doing so, it aired Wollstonecraft's various scandals, particularly her suicide attempts and her unwed motherhood. This exposed her to attacks which clouded her reputation for over a century. Did Godwin just lack discretion? It's not clear why he thought it wise to divulge the private details of Wollstonecraft's life, which had generated controversy enough while she was alive. The condemnations came in loud and swift. Horace Walpole called her a "hyena in petticoats" and American president John Adams referred to her as "this mad woman"—as "foolish" and "licentious." In a long, scathing response, a reviewer in the *Anti-Jacobin Review* referred to Wollstonecraft as a "concubine."

Memoirs is also strangely unconcerned with the child who has just been born. Although Godwin describes Wollstonecraft's labor and the extraction of the placenta in surprisingly graphic detail, Mary Shelley is never named and her gender is not mentioned. Godwin simply writes, "The child was born at twenty minutes after eleven at night." The child is otherwise omitted from the story of her own birth.

Mary grew up reading her mother's inspiring books but also encountering the terrible things written and said about her. Meanwhile, her father, to whom she was passionately devoted, was in his study writing books and launching a publishing house devoted to children's literature. He was aided in this endeavor by a woman he married four years after Wollstonecraft's death. His second wife—an editor, translator, and the mother of two fatherless children—had a furious temper, and she drove a wedge between Godwin and his daughter. Mary Shelley never warmed to her stepmother, the woman who took increasing control of Godwin's household.

Perhaps given confidence by her celebrity literary pedigree, however scandalous, and perhaps in retreat from her stepmother's domineering presence, Mary Shelley started writing at an early age. In her own words, "As a child I scribbled." She published her first book under her father's imprint, the Juvenile Library, when she was only eight. Her world was changing; women's literary output greatly increased in the early nineteenth century and a female writer was less of an exception. A woman writer, however, was still often viewed as an inexperienced dabbler at best. At worst, she was a threatening breach of the natural order, a deviator from her prescribed role as daughter, mother, wife, and biological procreator. Her books were her monstrous, illegitimate, ill-fated children.

Nineteenth-century authorship was bound up in ideas of masculinity. To be an author was to be an authority, to mastermind new creations, to birth them literarily, and to name them. In critic Edward Said's words, an author was "an increaser and thus a founder." Authorship was both production and possession. The author, who had been a mere scribe through long stretches of history, had become imbued with a sacred status, with godlike powers of inspired creation. In their 1979 feminist classic *The Madwoman in the Attic*, critics Sandra Gilbert and Susan Gubar argue that the author became in this era "a father, a progenitor, a procreator, an aesthetic patriarch whose pen is an instrument of generative power like his penis." The literary tradition was a lineage of fathers who imaginatively raised talented, exceptional sons, sons who assumed their inheritance and imagined the conquest of new frontiers. This was the Age of Enlightenment, of the elevation of human reason, implicit within which was the pursuit of human mastery—a mastery outwardly realized in imperialism and the horrors of the transatlantic slave trade.

What role would a young writing woman have had within this tradition? What would it mean to disrupt this patriarchal lineage and establish a female, matrilineal, creative line, one that wasn't just metaphorical but that was based on the full, raw, bodily experience of human childbirth? In the literary succession between Mary Wollstonecraft and Mary Shelley, the authority of the male author, the way in which he had dominated the literary tradition with his abstract birthing, was challenged. Mary thought back through her mother, not in terms of bodily memories but through the medium of books. Following in her mother's footsteps and growing up in the shadow of her mother's death, she would write one of the greatest birth myths of the modern era, one that subverted many inherited myths and many Enlightenment and Romantic ideas about human creativity and mastery. It remains a challenging testament to natality today.

Like many girls of her era, Mary lacked the classical education of many of her male peers. Girls who sought a rigorous curriculum had to find their own teachers, cobbling together a haphazard education at the feet of male family friends, neighbors, fathers, and husbands. And even when women found such pedagogues, they had to reckon with the fact that the tradition they encountered had occluded and even entirely excluded women's experiences, including pregnancy, childbirth, and motherhood. Their teachers also had different ideas about a writer's agency. For Percy Shelley, Mary's future husband and one of her primary intellectual tutors, poets were the "legislators," not the servants, of the world.

He, as legislator, would father Mary's five children, four of whom died young or in utero, in the taxed turmoil of her young, maternal, writer's body. She wrote in his shadow, referring to his mind as "far more cultivated" than her own. He supported her work and encouraged her writing, but by her own account, it was not with the belief that she would produce anything great, but so that he could "judge how far [she] possessed the promise of better things hereafter." He tutored her and edited her literary creations which shocked the world with their tragic and even monstrous account of an ambitious, liberated natality.

o o o

Mary Wollstonecraft Godwin met Percy Bysshe Shelley when she was sixteen. He was an Eton-educated member of the landed gentry, the heir to a large fortune, but he was also a rebel, an acolyte of both Godwin and Wollstonecraft and a disciple of the radical eighteenth-century philosophers who insisted on the intrinsically benevolent nature of humankind. He had begun visiting Godwin's house to discuss art and politics and, on one visit, he was taken by Godwin's most beloved daughter, a reserved, serious, silent girl with a pale face who in turn was drawn to his visionary eyes and reformatory dreams. They talked and Mary later claimed that he freed up her voice, allowing her to "communicate with unlimited freedom." He was, unfortunately, six years older than she was and he was already married to Harriet Westbrook, whom he had left at home with their firstborn child and a second on the way.

Soon after meeting, Mary and Percy traveled together to her mother's grave, where, at the site of Wollstonecraft's dead body, they read books and kindled their romance. Mary declared her love for him graveside, in her mother's spectral presence. He perceived her mother's shining light flooding through her. In her beauty, calm, freedom, and wisdom, he wrote later in a poem dedicated to her, she broke "the mortal chain / of Custom." The next day felt to him like his birthday; he was being reborn. They began planning a life together, a natal chain of creative unconventionality perhaps, but when they brought their plans home to her father, to their surprise Godwin, the radical, objected. He was outraged. He begged the young poet to spare his fair and spotless daughter.

Aware that this unsanctioned romance made Mary a social outcast, just as her mother had been, yet intent on pursuing their relationship, the pair fled London for Paris, bringing along Mary's younger stepsister and a stack of books. They began a fugitive period buoyed by their blossoming passions and the thrill of escape but also the painful rejections, scandal, and isolation. Godwin refused to see his daughter, and their relationship would never be fully repaired. But Mary and Percy still read Godwin's and Wollstonecraft's work devotedly, keeping themselves rooted in her family lineage, living out her parents' revolutionary ideas and devoting themselves to learning. (Percy taught Mary Greek; they'd eventually co-translate Plato's *Symposium*.) They were financially sustained by the money he extracted from his family, but they were nourished by her intellectual inheritance.

Their liberatory flight was stressful. They were constantly moving; Percy was on the run from creditors; they were short on money; and they slept in a series of squalid inns where, for instance, Mary felt a rat's cold paws stepping on her face at night. She grew moody. Percy's wife, Harriet, gave birth to her second child, a birth that strained his finances but seems not to have otherwise concerned him. Mary also witnessed in Europe the plundered and pillaged ruins the Napoleonic Wars had left behind. Mere months before their arrival in France, the Cossacks and the Austrian and Prussian armies had torn through the pastoral landscape, burning villages, killing children, raping women, and stealing livestock. Her mother and father had dreamed of revolution, but she saw with her own disillusioned eyes the costs of war, the suffering of innocent, defeated, and now starving people, and the scorched earth of the post-revolutionary period.

As they traveled, Mary felt increasingly weak and nauseated. Profoundly fatigued, she realized she had missed her period. Just before returning to England, still only sixteen, she finally faced the fact that she was pregnant. The pregnancy drew her away from Percy into her own exhaustion, and it drew Percy away from her into the company of her lively stepsister, whom many believe became his lover during Mary's first pregnancy. She'd been cast off by her father and cheated on by the man she was in love with. But she stayed in her dead mother's company, reading and rereading Wollstonecraft's works.

o o o

Two months before her due date, Mary went into labor. A doctor, who was likely the same physician who had attended to Mary Wollstonecraft through her puerperal fever, was called to her side and on February 22, 1815, a baby girl was born. Mary was seventeen, with her lover and stepsister by her side but with no one else offering their support. She drew her tiny newborn daughter to her breast, nursing her and hoping she would grow strong. But a couple of weeks later, before the child had even been named, Mary woke in the middle of the night to nurse her only to find her baby peacefully sleeping—a sleep that in the morning she discovered was the sleep of death.

"I was a mother and now am not," she wrote rather tersely. "It is hard to lose a baby." What had she done wrong? Why had this baby died? She started having repeated nightmares about her dead baby. "Dream that my little baby came to life again," she wrote in her journal, "that it had only been cold & that we rubbed it by the fire & it lived—I awake & find no baby—I think about the little thing all day." She was consumed by maternal guilt, by the question of whether she was at fault for this premature baby's death. Meanwhile, Shelley was writing lines like "Life, the great miracle, we admire not, because it is so miraculous." "What is life," he asked, and "what are we? Whence do we come? and whither do we go? Is birth the commencement, is death the conclusion of our being? What is birth and death?"

But despite her grief—and his grief—Mary tried to return to the world and to regenerate her romance with Percy. Several months after her baby's death, she was pregnant again. Sick again. Tired again. But this time they stayed in one place, renting a house in England where they read, wrote, and established the imaginative groundwork for both writers' most celebrated literary creations.

While Mary was pregnant, they read John Milton's *Paradise Lost* and were taken with Milton's rebellious, heroic Satan, an angel fallen from God's grace who found in his expulsion an individualistic freedom and the possibility of a self-making that had been denied to him in heaven. Like other Romantics, they saw Satan as a revolutionary, Promethean figure, a protester against a hierarchical tyrant God, and a symbol of their own disgraceful fallenness. "Better to reign in Hell," says Milton's Satan, "than serve in Heav'n." They, too, were discovering their own creative freedom on the wrong side of conventional Christian morality, and like Satan, the price they paid was banishment. Or maybe they were like Adam and Eve, cast out from the garden after eating the fruit of the tree of knowledge. Milton's *Paradise Lost* was a retelling of the Genesis story of humankind's disobedience, of an expulsion that was compounded by the punishment of childbirth for Eve.

As her baby gestated, Mary started to read about the horrors of the slave trade, now outlawed in England but still thriving in the Americas. She was still researching the slave trade when she went into labor for the second time. On January 24, 1816, a baby boy was born, and his parents named him William after his grandfather. Mary, now a mother for the second time, was still a teenager. To her relief, this baby survived and grew strong in the weeks and months after his birth.

But her mother's death and the events of the last few years—the pregnancies and births, the abandonments and attachments, the revolutionary hopes and dreams of a reasonable world and the realities of a messy, violent, human one—were about to coalesce in her imagination and be given a horrifying shape on the page as she conceived of and wrote *Frankenstein*, about an overly ambitious, Promethean creator–scientist who, driven maniacally in his quest to discover life's source, reanimates a corpse, making a living creature in his "workshop of filthy creation."

o o o

Mary took to motherhood, but London felt like a hostile place for the new parents. Her stepsister Claire convinced the couple to travel to Geneva to join their fellow poet Lord Byron, with whom she had become romantically entangled and by whom she'd soon be pregnant and promptly abandoned. At that time, Byron was one of the most famous men in Europe, a womanizing, outlaw poet whom one of his lovers called "mad, bad and dangerous to know." When baby William was only a few months old, the trio made the journey to Switzerland, passing through the snowy Alps and arriving on the verdant shores of Lake Geneva, where Milton himself had once stayed. There, the scandalized locals claimed, Byron, Shelley, Mary, and Claire set up a harem. In the London papers, the bohemian entourage became known as "the league of incest."

It rained incessantly that season and the friends, confined to the house, gathered around a fire at night and discussed the "principle of life." The men talked, and Mary sat silently listening. Was the birth of human beings just a natural process, rather than a divine act by God? Could a corpse, for instance, be reanimated by a human? Could a scientist make a person? Percy, a self-declared atheist, was more inclined to say yes, but Mary thought no. It was partly that she still believed in God, but partly that her experiences had dimmed her view of human nature and had thrown into doubt humankind's ability to control such mysterious experiences as birth. If humans were in control, then surely her mother wouldn't have died giving birth to her and her newborn baby girl would still be alive.

On one now legendary night that summer, it was still raining; thunder roared and lightning electrified the skies. They gathered again, reading German ghost stories aloud until Byron declared, "We will each write a ghost story." Mary went to sleep that night and over the following days, she tried to dream up a story. But she couldn't think of anything. She wrote later that she "felt that blank incapability of invention which is the greatest misery of authorship, when dull Nothing replies to our anxious invocations." Nothing comes from nothing. Everything that exists emerges out of something, she believed. "Invention," she wrote, "does not con-sist in creating out of void, but out of chaos; the materials must, in the first place, be afforded." Through invention, a human cre-ator can give formless shapes new forms, but he cannot create their substance.

At last, one night, she lay awake, sleepless with a waking night-mare. She envisioned a "pale student of unhallowed arts kneeling beside the thing he had put together." Suddenly the hideous "thing" comes to life and, horrified, the student of unhallowed arts, like a negligent god or a selfish father, promptly abandons his own creation.

This, in a nutshell, would become the plot of the book she was about to write: *Frankenstein: Or, The Modern Prometheus*, a tragic realization of humanity's natal dreams.

o   o   o

As Mary Shelley worked on her horror story, her half-sister Fanny Imlay took a deadly overdose of laudanum. Left behind by Mary and Claire, Fanny had borne the brunt of her stepmother's anger and had grown increasingly depressed. Two months later, Percy's first wife, Harriet, newly pregnant again (by another man this time) and struggling to raise Percy's two children on her own, drowned herself. Days later, Mary and Percy quickly married. During these months she wrote and gestated, grieved and worried, edited her work and cared for her young child. The writing of the book, like the gestation of her baby, took her nine months.

As Mary Shelley's recent biographer Charlotte Gordon notes, "The significance of the novel's gestation was not lost on Mary." Mary "referred to the book as her 'offspring' or 'progeny.'" The act of writing it was a "dilation." Mary recognized in the writing process the parallels with both her own birth and the birthing of her children. It was "as though she wrote the tale for herself," Gordon writes, "becoming both author and audience, creator and created, mother and daughter, inventor and destroyer."

About a month after *Frankenstein* was accepted for publication, Mary went into labor and gave birth to her second daughter, Clara. Mary struggled to produce enough milk, but the baby was healthy. *Frankenstein* was published anonymously in January of 1818, without any author credited, as was common with books written by women in this period. It came out to both savage criticism and surprising commercial success. Most readers assumed a man had written it, possibly Percy Bysshe Shelley.

But despite the book's success, Mary's bad-luck streak continued. In September of that year, little Clara died in Mary's lap, after
spiking a high fever and contracting dysentery. The following year,
Mary was pregnant again, but during that pregnancy, in June, little
William died from a fever at age three. Another child, Percy, was
born in November of 1819 in the wake of these deaths, after only
two short hours of labor. He would be the only child of Mary's who
survived his infancy and early childhood, and he would outlive his
mother. In the three years that followed, however, Mary nearly bled
to death after a miscarriage, surviving only because Percy Shelley
placed her unconscious in a tub of ice. Mary could not return that
favor and save him a few months later when, in the summer of 1822,
he drowned in a reckless boating accident. At the age of twenty-four,
Mary had alienated her birth family, lost four children, survived her
husband's death, and written what would become a literary classic.

Frankenstein is shadowed by those dizzying, broken family lineages, by those tenuous new lives and devastating deaths. The story
began, in her account, with the idea that "perhaps a corpse would be
re-animated." What would it mean to create life where there was no
life, to create something from nothing? "Frightful must it be," she
wrote, as if answering that specific question, "for supremely frightful would be the effect of any human endeavour to mock the stupen-
dous mechanism of the Creator of the world." She continues, "His
success would terrify the artist; he would rush away from his odi-
ous handiwork, horror-stricken. He would hope that, left to itself,
the slight spark of life which he had communicated would fade . . .
would subside into dead matter."

The dream of reanimating a corpse comes to Victor Frankenstein, a man who grew up in a happy, loving family, surrounded by
friends, but who turns obsessively in young adulthood into solitary

study of the natural sciences, intent on discovering the causation behind all life and neglecting his family and the natural world around him. He works on his project with relentless and engrossed fury for two years, barely sleeping or resting, as he gathers dead limbs from graves and tortures living animals, trying to discover the secret of life. Discovering such a secret would put a miraculous, astonishing power into his hands, he realizes. He meticulously plans every detail in his workshop. "I had selected his features as beautiful," he says. "Beautiful! Great God!"

The moment his creature comes alive, Frankenstein sees that he is not beautiful. He is hideous. His dream of beauty dissipates, and breathless horror and disgust fill Victor Frankenstein's heart. How could his beautiful form become a monster the moment the miracle occurs, the instant life enters the body? What does this say about life itself? The creature is a motherless human life engineered by ambitious male inventors, born without lineage, language, or any tradition. What ancestry would such a being think back through? There is none of Virginia Woolf's fertilizing of female and male energies in his creation, no unique sexual charge. He has emerged from the singular chamber of a male mind.

Frankenstein's instant horror feels like a cruel betrayal of the creature he has created, however disgusting or distorted that creation might be. The scientist flees his workshop. The rest of the novel is the story of the abandoned creature, made rapacious by his intolerable solitude, stalking his creator, seeking revenge upon him wherever he goes, until the creator finally reverses the direction of the chase, abandoning himself entirely to the pursuit of and intended destruction of his creature. This chase leads to the earth's icy Arctic reaches, where the novel ends with the monster's sad, satisfied, yet remorseful soliloquy delivered over Frankenstein's dead body.

o o o

Who is Mary in the novel and who is Percy Shelley? Who is Godwin and who is Wollstonecraft? Who, furthermore, is Adam and who is Eve? Who is Prometheus and who is Satan? Who is the wronged and who is the wrongdoer? Who is the creator and who is in control of creation? Interpreters have offered different identifications over the years.

Perhaps the monster is Mary Shelley, the abandoned child who killed her mother, her creator, in her coming into being. Or maybe Mary is the Promethean creator, whose books were the destructive, monstrous creations that came alive at the cost of her children. Or could both Frankenstein and his monster be Eve, dramatized in Mary Shelley's divided consciousness? The novel has retained its aesthetic, imaginative power for readers for two centuries now, perhaps due to its refusal to look away from the hard questions around both birth and death, but also because of these flexible, riddle-like characterizations. The characters bleed into one another, into the real people they were inspired by, and into the mythic figures of Adam, Eve, Satan, and Prometheus that haunt the novel, and they collectively resist easy classifications. Both the angels of our nature and the devils are implicated in human creativity and in the birthing of another human being.

Gender is also hard to pin down. Both Frankenstein and his creation are presented as male, but the creature's coming alive is bracketed between the deaths of Frankenstein's mother and his wife. Mary roots the story in the bodies of generative and yet vulnerable women, even if a male Frankenstein usurps the role of the creative, birthing mother. Frankenstein conceives of his humanoid after the death of his own mother from scarlet fever and his subsequent departure from home. Then, just as his creature comes alive, he has a vision of his future wife Elizabeth walking down the street in "the bloom of health." He goes to kiss her and her lips "became livid with the hue of death." "I thought," says Frankenstein, "that I held the corpse of my dead mother in my arms; a shroud enveloped her form, and I saw the grave-worms crawling in the folds of the flannel." Years later, when his creature strangles his bride on their wedding night, after having already murdered his brother and his best friend, Frankenstein has finally lost everything worth living for and he becomes exclusively set on pursuing and destroying his tor-mentor. But he fails; his tormentor, his creation, destroys him.

Mary Shelley subtitled the novel "The Modern Prometheus." Prometheus was a Titan, a trickster god who in some of the ancient Greek accounts created humans and gave them fire, a gift through which they could create their civilization. But for his creativity, he was punished. He was tied to a rock and Zeus, the supreme Greek god, came in the form of an eagle each day and ate out his liver. Every night it grew back, and the next day the torture was repeated. The Romantics revived Prometheus for their modern world; he became a symbol of the tortured artist, the human rival of a heavenly Creator.

Mary Shelley saw in Prometheus something else, too: an allegory of the birthing mother. Prometheus is only a half-god—a Titan— and he is tortured by the supreme god for usurping his authority. Frankenstein is similarly punished for taking on the activities of the Creator, a Christian-like God in the novel whose authority is in question. Mary Shelley wrote many decades before Nietzsche declared the death of God, arguing that we are his murderers; even so, questions about God's existence—his authority, his role in the miracle of life, his ability to control or take responsibility for what he has created—haunt the novel. And, of course, in the novel, the created creature murders the powerful being that created him.

If God created Victor Frankenstein and the world he inhabits, isn't he then also the creator of Frankenstein's monster? Or is human creativity a transgression, like Eve's eating the apple in the Garden of Eden, an exercise of free will with severe repercussions? Similarly, if Frankenstein made the monster, is he responsible for everything the monster does, or is the monster gifted, like humans, with a free will that puts upon him the full weight of his actions?

Frankenstein's monster refuses to accept the blame for the destruction he has caused. The novel opens with Adam's haunting words to God in Milton's *Paradise Lost*:

> *Did I request thee, Maker, from my clay*
> *To mould me Man, did I solicit thee*
> *From darkness to promote me?*

The monster indicts Frankenstein for his role as creator of his monstrosity: "You accuse me of murder; and yet you would, with a satisfied conscience, destroy your own creature. Oh, praise the eternal justice of man!" Whose fault is the creature's monstrosity?

Was it Mary Shelley's fault that her coming into life killed her mother? Is she a murderer? Is she responsible for the death of her own children whom she has outlived? Or was this part of God's plan? If the latter, what kind of god would destroy his newborn creation?

o o o

Perhaps the book's staying power also derives from its broader, social, and political ambitions. Mary Shelley's birth myth confronted the most pressing and fraught realities of her day: conquest, imperialism, and colonialism—the heady dreams of discovery that she could see were riddled with violent, Promethean impulses.

Many have seen the monster, for instance, as a symbol for the slave in the transatlantic slave trade, a human born out of dangerous European dreams about the mastery of nature, an aberrant being who possesses more moral authority than the morally deformed creator who authors his humanity. The dominion of one human being over another in the most elemental realities of birth, life, and death locks all characters in the novel into a tidal wave of destruction; they are all doomed by Frankenstein's Eve-like mistake. His attempt at discovering the cause of all life is like Eve's stealing and eating the fruit on the tree of knowledge.

The age of discovery frames the book from beginning to end. Frankenstein's story is nestled narratively within a sea voyager's letters back home to his sister, after he discovers Frankenstein near death, afloat on an iceberg in the Arctic. The discoverer is a failed poet who lived for a full year in "a paradise of my own creation" before abandoning his art and turning to mathematics, medicine, and the natural sciences. His curiosity and love of marvels propel him toward "a part of the world never before visited . . . a land never before imprinted by the foot of man." But he is lonely out on the frozen seas, in charge of his ship, and he is clear-eyed enough to see that what he wishes to acquire through knowledge is a problematic dominion over elemental forces. This dominative drive results in his fractured consciousness. He experiences the most profound human sorrows, which awaken him to the beauty of nature but also to how he is subject to her accidents. This makes him determined not to accept his subjectivity but to transcend the earth through his own ingenuity.

Just as it did for Arendt, Nietzsche, and Wollstonecraft, natality entails an anchoring on the earth for Mary Shelley. Like Wollstonecraft, Mary Shelley also problematizes a turn away from home and from the close kinship networks that bind one there. Hannah

Arendt was steadfastly committed to the public realm, to free people coming together out of their individual privacies to create new realities, but Mary Shelley offers a more cautionary tale about those public, dreamed-of creations. Arendt imagined a politics rooted in abstract births, but Mary's politics were tied closer to the home and to the births that took place there. As a survivor of many desertions, she was sensitive to the private homes and families those public people leave behind to come together to re-create their societies.

Like Wollstonecraft, she saw a maternal, domestic nurturance as central to the health of any civilization, and not just to individual children. If humans had not allowed their own ambitions to interfere with their domestic affections, Frankenstein himself admits, "Greece had not been enslaved, Caesar would have spared his country, America would have been discovered more gradually, and the empires of Mexico and Peru had not been destroyed."

If the absence of the parent destabilizes human life, the absence of a child in a parent's life creates its own sublime terror. "I loved to imagine futurity," Mary Shelley wrote in a letter, but she confesses that after her children's deaths, when she tries to imagine the future, she can only envision a dead child. "What should I do then," she asks and then responds, "never does the idea of peaceful futurity intrude itself . . ." She saw no peaceful future on her horizons.

Four years after Percy's death, and still haunted by the deaths of her babies, Mary Shelley published her dystopian novel *The Last Man*. Set in the twenty-first century, the novel narrates a deadly pandemic that spreads across Europe, killing most of its inhabitants. A man bears witness to the "universal wreck," and observes that "I lived upon an earth whose diminished population a child's arithmetic might number." As the pandemic progresses, he encounters among the shrinking ranks of survivors a mother who has given birth amid this apocalypse, after the plague killed her husband. Her child's birth "restored her to the cruel reality of things," but it also gave her "an object for whom to preserve at once life and reason." That drive to preserve the child's life amid the devastation drives her to fanaticism, and it makes her a desperate hostage to life. Before long, however, even her fanaticism can't save her. She and her child are killed too.

Finally, only a last man is left. He sails around the world on a "seedless ocean" like a world explorer with nothing left to discover. "The world was empty; mankind was dead." Yet the man holds out some hope. What he is hoping for isn't quite clear. "They were all to me," he laments, thinking of his lost friends and family members. "I would have wound myself like ivy inextricably round them, so that the same blow might destroy us." "I called myself hopeless," he confesses, "yet still I hoped." The novel ends with those three staccato words: "the LAST MAN."

Mary Shelley was not the last man. She survived her private losses and lived through a history within which no apocalypse struck. She lived out the remainder of her years like that mother in *The Last Man* whom birth had acquainted with "the cruel reality of things" while also giving her "an object for whom to preserve at once life and reason." In her remaining years, she preserved her own life and reason and her surviving child lived, too. Then, after a decade-long struggle with a brain tumor, she died in 1851 at the age of fifty-three. Her one surviving child buried her lovingly between her parents.

Mary Shelley was a natal thinker, but she reminds us that natality can be infused with a sober, bitter wisdom. What she so painfully and powerfully depicted about natality is how we ultimately don't control birth, despite the scientific advancements that have attempted to enlarge our procreative powers. We don't get to choose which new lives arrive in our lives, nor who survives. What is about to be born might be, instead of an innocent newborn baby, or instead of a divine savior, what William Butler Yeats describes in his famous poem "The Second Coming" as a "rough beast" who "slouches towards Bethlehem to be born." The newborn's life sets in motion a sequence of events which include death—our deaths, anyone's deaths. As Frankenstein reflects: "Thus strangely are our souls constructed, and by such slight ligaments are we bound to prosperity or ruin."

To Be the Instrument

In the 1990s, American academic and memoirist Saidiya Hartman traveled to Ghana to trace the history of the transatlantic slave trade, to understand how so many lives had been destroyed and how slaves had been born. The trip wasn't just an academic research project; it was personally motivated, too. Hartman wanted to "excavate a wound" from her personal past as an American descendant of slaves. Who were her ancestors? Where did they come from and what were their histories? Visiting the forts and storehouses, the slave markets and fortified towns, the mercantile centers and the communities throughout Ghana that had been so thoroughly pillaged, she looked for evidence of broken ancestries, trying to understand how those family lines had been ruptured. She titled the book that emerged from these travels *Lose Your Mother: A Journey Along the Atlantic Slave Route*: her testament to birth, disrupted mother-lines, and loss.

Her thinking back through her slave mothers takes her not to a family house, village, or tribe—but instead to a grotesque nativity scene, an underworld lodged in the bowels of the earth. She had been drawn to Ghana primarily for one reason: the country has more prisons, dungeons, and slave pens than any other West African nation. Dark, buried cells play a particular role in her account of slavery and its lost mothers. "Every tale of creation I had ever read," she writes, "began in a place like this—in the underworld, in the bowels of the earth, in the gloom of man's prehistory. The cradle of life bore an uncanny resemblance to the grave."

The place she is referring to is Cape Coast Castle, a structure built in 1674 by the British to warehouse slaves—one of the two largest castles on Africa's Gold Coast. When I hear "castle," I think of upward, ornamental spires, but this castle burrows downward; the slave pens were built deep in the earth, with vaulted cellar chambers designed to impede escape and rebellion. Visiting the castle's vaults, Hartman sees a tomb, a dank cellar with perspiring walls that she describes as the earth's open wound. The floors of the dungeons look like dirt, but they're covered in inches and inches of human remains—dead skin, dried blood, caked feces.

Surprisingly, the British didn't see the dungeons as tombs. They imagined them as wombs. As the Royal Africa Company and the Company of Merchants saw it, "the dungeon was a womb in which the slave was born." In those cellars with their oozing walls, in those sites of death and disease where slaves slept, made love, gave birth, and died in their waste, stolen people were transformed into slaves; they were forced to shed their pasts and leave behind their natal lands to inaugurate their new lives as commodities. If the dungeons were wombs, then the Middle Passage was the birth canal, Hartman argues, through which the slaves journeyed outward into new lives, a new world. Instead of records of births in church registers, family diary entries, or birth certificates issued by the state, for slaves one finds only records of sale. With each financial transaction, a slave was born into a new family and given a new place of belonging and a new name. "Gestational language," Hartman argued elsewhere, "has been key to describing the world-making and world-breaking capacities of racial slavery" in which the "master dreams of future increase."

"Be fruitful and multiply," says God in the Hebrew Bible, but that fruitfulness and multiplication meant human breeding for Hartman's ancestors. A biblical drama was replayed in the transatlantic slave trade, with God replaced by human actors. Slave traders became the Creators. "Adam and Eve," Hartman tells us, were born not in paradise but "in this filthy pit": "So the British called the first man and woman plucked from the dungeon and bound aboard the slave ship, replaying the drama of birth and expulsion in the Africa trade." The pain of childbirth was God's punishment for an erring humanity in Genesis, but this origin story includes no crime committed by the subjects being punished. Neither does it include an original Edenic soil out of which the new creations were sculpted. Instead, it's just "blood and shit" that "ushered us into the world."

There is a terrible irony in describing the dungeons as wombs, because these cells marked the place of separation from networks of kin. A slave is someone who has lost her mother. A slave is a person whose child will likely be taken from her, transferred to a different lineage upon birth. That child's children will in turn be taken from her. They, too, will lose their mother and their children will likewise be stolen from them. Slave mothers can grieve the loss of their children, but they cannot protect them.

The slaves held in the dungeons of Cape Coast Castle left no written records. In an era when literacy was spreading, slaves were routinely forbidden any education. We don't know what words they would have used to describe those holding cells. Perhaps they too would have used the language of wombs and birth. Or maybe they would have called them tombs, seeing in those dungeons only endings. The lived experiences of these slaves have been lost to time.

Except, of course, in those very rare instances when they weren't.

o o o

In about 1797, the year Mary Shelley was born and Mary Wollstonecraft died, an enslaved woman was born in Ulster County, New York, about ninety miles north of New York City, in a landscape of rolling hills, small lakes, and sandy soil. She would never know her precise birthday and she was born without a last name, although several of her masters' surnames were attached to her and her parents in various records. For over four decades, she was known as Isabella, but in middle age, she renamed herself Sojourner Truth. As Truth, she would be reborn, becoming an itinerant preacher and, eventually, one of the most famous black American women of the nineteenth century. If slavery as an institution involved remaking people, she provides a rare example of a slave's testimony of her own remaking. She would spread a message of abolition, temperance, and women's rights, infused with the language of birth. Articulating new conceptions of human natality, she imagined how birth's "world-breaking" dimensions could be mined for its "world-making" potential.

Like the day of her birth, the exact place of Isabella's birth was never recorded. But locals in Ulster County have identified cottages along Rondout Creek, a winding tributary of the Hudson River in the rural township of Rosendale, in one of which she is believed to have been born. The town is full of oaks and wild roses, blue herons and icy caves. When Isabella was still a child, hydraulic cement was discovered in the ground, and by the second half of the nineteenth century, five thousand townspeople would be employed in the cement industry. Rosendale would eventually produce 50 percent of the US's natural cement. Isabella worked household jobs, but she also was tasked with working that cement-rich land.

She didn't know the day or time of her birth, but she knew her parents: James and Elizabeth (known to many as either Betsy or Mau Mau Bett), both slaves of Colonel Johannis Hardenbergh, a prosperous early settler of the region. She was the youngest of her parents' ten to twelve children and she was born into their middle age, after they had experienced countless losses. Her father had had two wives before her mother, and both had been sold off. Her siblings had also been sold off before she could remember them. She grew up knowing only one of them, an older brother named Peter, though she had lived with two others. As Truth narrated it, after having risen with the birds and made a fire, Isabella's unsuspecting brother had called out to his mother that her fire was ready. But before she could come, an old-fashioned sleigh rode in through the snowy landscape and its occupants attempted to snatch the boy, who ran inside and hid under a bed. They caught him and put him in the sleigh where his sister was locked in a box, before riding away. Isabella's siblings were three and five when this happened. Was this kidnapping any worse than being sold on the auction block? Truth doesn't say.

Her parents kept her lost siblings alive through stories that were never written down until Truth dictated them to her amanuensis, Olive Gilbert, a white abolitionist, in the 1840s, when she was already in her midforties. Without that dictation, these stories would never have been recorded.

Truth remembered an affectionate family, one bound together by a love that was unimaginable to their masters and to a wider white American culture. Her mother, after her work was done for the day, would "sit down under the sparkling vault of heaven, and calling her children to her, would talk to them of the only Being that could effectually aid or protect them." She taught her children the Lord's Prayer and assured them that God would come to their aid if they asked him to. He would come to them when they were beaten or poorly treated or when they got into trouble. They just needed to pray to him, be good, and remain obedient. She encouraged her children to look up at the stars, at a moon that was the same moon that looked down upon the family members who had been sold off and taken away from them. Her mother would "strengthen and brighten the chain of family affection, which she trusted extended itself sufficiently to connect the widely scattered members of her precious flock." But Isabella would often also find her strengthening, brightening mother in tears, her heart crucified afresh by those memories.

These memories, for all the trauma with which they were inscribed, were held sacred by Isabella. Her parents, who had been afforded their own cottage while still enslaved, and who had independently worked a plot of land, would see their situation deteriorate when Colonel Hardenbergh died. They lost their cottage and were moved into a dismal basement where men, women, and children slept together on a floor of hay covering wooden boards laid over a wet, uneven, muddy earth—an underground dungeon reminiscent of those in Cape Coast Castle. They were denied any basic comforts, Truth believed, because slaveowners maintained their mastery through a warped imaginary in which the people they owned didn't need or even desire such comforts. They were understood to be inhumanly strong and yet innately inferior.

The auction day came, and the dead colonel's slaves, horses, and cattle were collectively "put under the hammer." Isabella was sold for a hundred dollars, alongside some sheep. Her parents, too old to be of any value, were granted their freedom to absolve their owners of the burden of caring for them in their old age. Her mother lived for only a few more years, and Isabella was able to visit her a few times before she died in a fit of palsy in that dank cellar. After her mother's death, her father was left "penniless, weak, lame, and nearly blind . . . alone in the world, with no one to aid, comfort, or console him." Isabella saw him only a couple more times before his death. She later remembered him visiting her at her cruel new master's house. He had journeyed through the snow to see her, and when he departed through the gate, he left footprints in the snow. Every day, for as long as that snow lasted, she visited his footprints and thereby kept alive his spectral bodily presence as she prayed to God to help them. Her father, however, did not live long. "This faithful slave," she'd narrate, "this deserted wreck of humanity, was found on his miserable pallet, frozen and stiff in death."

These early losses shaped how Truth thought about and spoke about birth in the years ahead. One of the phrases that she repeats in this part of her narration of her childhood is "care for." Her family promised that they would care for one another, although they lacked the means to offer much more than their expressions of faithful love.

Isabella was sold several times before she was bought by John Dumont, whose family she would live with for sixteen years, during which time she would fall in love with an enslaved man who was punished severely for his relationship with her. At the age of seventeen or eighteen, she married another slave owned by the Dumonts, a man named Thomas who had already lost two wives. Living with the Dumonts, married to Thomas, she would give birth to five children, four of whom are known to have lived and accompanied her out of slavery. She was beaten with some regularity by Dumont, to whom she developed a strange, painful, and enduring attachment, and, it is widely believed, she was sexually abused by his wife, Sally, whom she hated. Male masters' sex with and rape of female slaves was an integral part of chattel slavery, but homosexual relations were so shameful and unspeakable in the nineteenth century that Sojourner Truth only hints at what happened in her narrative.

A new law enacted by the state of New York in 1809 allowed slaves to marry, own property, and transfer this property to one another. Marriage made slaves' children legitimate, a legitimacy that was new to a population that had been collectively seen as bastard children, and the law forbade the separation of families. But the idea of a family bound by romantic love and imbued with a Victorian domesticity, with an angel mother sacrificially attending, would rarely define the slave family. Isabella may have been forced to marry Thomas, a man she never professed any great love for; her birthing of children certainly increased the Dumonts' property, at little cost to them. Her children would remain indentured longer than she would, and although she lived with her daughters at the time of her death and remained connected to her children throughout their lives, they were seldom if ever all together again after she was freed.

Despite these early familial losses—or perhaps because of them—Truth would find in birth great creative possibilities for the remaking of oneself and one's own world, articulating a very original and powerful account of human natality.

o o o

Birth, maternity, mothers' bodies, the dependence of infancy, nursing, care, nurture—these were all critical themes evoked by Sojourner Truth at key moments when she became a celebrated figure in the most significant reform movements of her day: abolition, women's rights, and temperance. Birth in all its physicality and spiritual, creative depths would be a recurrent theme for her as she traveled the country as an itinerant preacher, but in her *Narrative*, she shared few details about her own experiences birthing her children. We hear nothing about how long the labor took, what placenta remained or was delivered alongside her babies, whether she experienced fevers or excessive bleeding, if her children were born before or after their due dates, what it was like to hold her newborn children's bodies for the first time, whether she experienced miscarriages between these births, if she dreamed of her children, or how involved her husband was in their lives. Through these same years, across the Atlantic, Mary Shelley was simultaneously conceiving, birthing, or burying her children, and we have her own private accounts and those of family members, friends, the state, journalists, and the famous writers who corroborated, elucidated, or expanded upon the details she chose to share. While Mary Shelley and her mother had struggled to write, publish, and be read seriously, Isabella and her family members were illiterate and legally unrecognized as anything other than property. Although Isabella would eventually become a distinctly public figure, her children's births, like hers, were never recorded. To be born a slave, she'd later believe, was to be born not fully alive. Such a birth entailed a living death sentence.

Unlike most of Mary Shelley's children, most of Isabella's lived. Nell Irvin Painter, one of Truth's biographers, lists Isabella's children as follows: "Diana, born about 1815; Peter, 1821; Elizabeth, 1825; and Sophia, about 1826. The fifth, perhaps named Thomas, may have died in infancy or childhood and may have been born between Diana and Peter."

Isabella, to her later horror, rejoiced at the time "in being permitted to be the instrument of increasing the property of her oppressors!" Her amanuensis challenged readers of the *Narrative* to imagine what it would be like to proudly and willingly lay one's own children on the altar of slavery. She reminds her audience, lest they rush to judgment, that a slave wasn't considered a mother; she was mere chattel, and the pride and duty of chattel was to produce more chattel, to contribute to the master's increase. It was only in her freedom that Sojourner Truth could become, belatedly, a mother and a woman, Olive Gilbert wrote. At the time, slaves were considered male, and women were all white.

Years later, Sojourner Truth would look back on that altar of slavery where she willingly laid her innocent, newborn children, and on her own ignorance and state of degradation, as on the "dark imagery of a fitful dream."

Between 1826 and 1827, soon after the birth of her youngest, Sophia, she managed to work her way to freedom, taking her newborn baby with her in one arm and some clothes and provisions wrapped in a handkerchief in the other. She left her other children and her husband behind, as they were still legally bound to the Dumonts. In her freedom, she lived and worked as a single woman and single mother, never again marrying and never having any more children, perhaps suggesting that those five conceptions and births weren't volitional acts she was ready or willing to repeat. Although she had no more children as a free woman, childbirth would provide inspiration for her ideas about freedom as she remade herself and tried to reform the "moral gutter" of nineteenth-century American life.

In one of the only testimonies provided by her children of the family's early life with their mother, the picture is tender. Diana, her oldest, remembered sitting with her mother and siblings in a cabin on the Dumont property, before a fire, as her mother mended clothes and told them of her dream that they would one day all live together in their own home. Isabella, by her own account, took her babies with her to the fields where she worked, sticking them in a basket which she hung low enough in a tree for another child to rock it, but high enough that she wouldn't need to bend when she went to nurse her children throughout the day. She appears to have been a loving mother, but she also admits to having beaten her children when they cried out in their hunger for bread, knowing that the bread they wanted wasn't theirs to take and not wanting to raise thieves.

Once freed, after almost thirty years as a slave, Isabella never looked back on those years with anything other than outrage and great pain. It took her decades to heal from the rawest wounds of her enslavement, to the degree that she ever fully healed. In her early years as a free woman, she lacked confidence and entered into exploitative relationships, enduring more physical and sexual abuse. But she also exhibited remarkable courage. In one of the first acts that made her a significant historical figure, very soon after her emancipation, she successfully sued a wealthy white man for the illegal sale of her five-year-old son to Alabama, where he was mercilessly beaten, before his new master was forced to return him. *"I'll have my child again."* "I must have my child." She had repeated such phrases to the family of her son's captor. But she was also whispering them to God, whom she believed "sees the end from the beginning, and controls the results."

God was for her an omnipotent being whom she understood as the Creator of all things great and small, including herself; she was a part of God's creation. "God," she'd later say, "is the great house that will hold all his children." In this sense, God was like a mother's body. This understanding gave her strength and hope. Jesus, whom she understood as a spirit standing between her and God, had the "same spirit that was in our first parents, Adam and Eve, in the beginning, when they came from the hand of their Creator." She grew in her faith during these difficult years, and was drawn into fiery, abolitionist Christian communities where she gained a sense of her own prophetic purpose. But first she would need to be reborn.

○ ○ ○

On June 1, 1843, Isabella woke, packed some clothes in a pillowcase, put two shillings in her purse, and left the home where she was living as a free woman in New York City, having made the decision to travel east, out to Long Island. "The Spirit calls me there, and I must go," she said. Before leaving, she informed the woman of the house that her name was now Sojourner. She'd later add a last name: Truth. Sojourner Truth: an apt name for an itinerant preacher, which she committed herself to being, and the name history remembers as hers.

At around this time, she became curious about the Bible, a book she liked hearing read aloud. She preferred children as readers, as they would repeat verses when asked, and, unlike adults, they refrained from adding their own commentary. She wanted to be her own interpreter. One might expect that she'd have been drawn to Exodus, but instead she was particularly fascinated by the first chapters of Genesis, the stories of God's creation of the world and of its first inhabitants. She later described her departure from New York in biblical terms, drawing on the story of Lot's wife: she fled a wicked city, a second Sodom clouded over with blue smoke, determined never to look back for fear that, like Lot's wife, she would turn into a pillar of salt. She left behind her painful memories and what she understood as her own sinfulness, and although her life path took many twists and turns, with intermittent periods of rootedness, she kept her new name until her death and remained an itinerant preacher, testifying to the power of the Holy Spirit for the rest of her life. In that sense, she never looked back, although the contents of her sermons were the stories of her childhood and her three decades of enslavement. Her new self's message contained the story of Isabella.

This renaming and exodus represented a rebirth for her, marking her passage into a new life dedicated to "testifying of the hope that was in her." She left on Pentecost, a day of baptism in the Holy Spirit that marks the advent of a messianic age. But the role of birth is contradictory in her actions. She left her children, the bodily proof of her physical birthing, alone in that wicked city when she traveled east. She would reconnect with them before long, but for a couple of months they had no idea where their mother had gone, and they feared for her sanity and safety. Her children remained connected to her throughout their lives, but family life was never her exclusive focus. Alongside her family relationships, she maintained a wide web of friends, acquaintances, admirers, and fellow seekers, as she devoted herself to the social and political concerns of a wider public realm. As her friend Frances W. Titus put it, "Sojourner, robbed of her own offspring, adopted her race." And yet her public, preaching self delivered a message about birth, that most private act—a message full of natality.

Her rebirth was spiritual, but it was also a rebirth into a personhood with a mission on the earth. A fervid, Second Adventist excitement about the coming end of the world, a day of judgment, and the salvation of true believers was reaching its height at the time. Sojourner Truth participated in Adventist communities and was shaped by them, but she also scolded those for whom a Pentecostal rebirth represented an escape from the world. She grounded herself in the world, in God's material creation. Climbing one day onto a stump, she gathered her "children," as she called the Adventists, around her and "with the tones of a kind mother" told them to watch and to pray. Observe the world as it is, and only then address God. The people she spoke to craved a quick transformation, the imminent coming of a new age, but she emphasized staying rather than escaping. "If the Lord comes and burns," she told them, "I am not going away; *I* am going to stay here and *stand the fire* . . . And Jesus will walk with me through the fire, and keep me from harm."

She declared herself a "self-made woman." Although she remained poor for most of her life, she became famous and was often near the center of action. She met presidents and other politicians; she was known and celebrated by many of the most important historical figures of the period: Frederick Douglass, Elizabeth Cady Stanton, Abraham Lincoln, William Lloyd Garrison, Harriet Beecher Stowe, Harriet Tubman, and many others. But her spiritual rebirth wasn't an abdication of Isabella, her old self, or of the horrors she had experienced in her chattelized body. It entailed using that same body to speak, to travel, and to spread a message, person to person, about what Isabella had experienced and to advocate the causes of women's rights, abolition, and spiritualism.

o o o

Sojourner Truth's physical body is mentioned in nearly every account recorded, from her own dictated *Narrative* to the newspaper articles and personal letters she appeared in—written by white men, white women, black men, and other black women. She is described as "a tall imposing figure, [with] a strong voice," "dignified," with a "finely molded form" of "grand height and graceful, wavy movements." She was reportedly close to six feet tall, with a deep, masculine voice and a mangled hand.

Many have noted that this focus on a black woman's body rhetorically reenacts the sizing up and objectification of a female slave on the auction block, where her body was understood to be all there was to her: its strength or weaknesses, its youth or old age, its procreative, laboring potential. If men have long been associated with the abstract realm of ideas and higher forms, women's bodies have, again, long represented a more carnal physicality. This physicality was particularly accentuated when it came to slave women's bodies.

Truth's genius and originality are rooted in her refusal to deny that physicality, to refute her objectification, and to try and grasp at some pure, abstract realm. Instead, she found new, unexplored, regenerative, imaginative, and moral resources within the clichés, stereotypes, and condemnations applied to her. She handed out small photos of herself, standing or seated, like business cards. On the bottom of the photo in her favorite card is the aphorism: "I Sell the Shadow to Support the Substance." She supported the substance by seeing dimensions of embodiment that others may have not considered, but also through her quick wit and original intelligence. She was sarcastic; many of her statements have a tongue-in-cheek quality. The intensity of her speaking style was softened by winks and smiles. She had a biting, common-sense humor that cut through her audience's prejudices, even as it softened the edge of her critiques and drew listeners to her. We can see the many ways she articulated such reversals in a speech she gave at a women's rights convention in Akron, Ohio, in 1851. It was first recorded by her friend and host Marius Robinson, the secretary of the convention, and revised and published by Frances Dana Gage twelve years later.

Robinson starts by commenting on Truth's "powerful form" and her "strong and truthful tones." In her first words, as she came to the platform, she confirmed her physical power. "I have as much muscle as any man," she said. "I am as strong as any man." That strength could be used as a bargaining chip; her strength entitled her to equal rights, she claimed. If she could do a man's work, she should be paid like a man.

Having affirmed her physical strength, she launched into the example of Eve, the emblematic representation of women's sinfulness with her carnal, uncontrollable desires, the woman who had single-handedly brought childbirth in all its physical agony upon humanity and who is eternally responsible for all the fallenness that came after her. But Truth saw a bright side to the story. If Eve had made an epic mistake, setting the world wrong by eating the forbidden fruit, she must also have the capacity to "set it right side up again." In Eve she saw a woman's earth-shattering and world–re-creating agency. Women were actors capable of changing their worlds.

Then, she made a provocative observation about the incarnation and Jesus's miraculous birth. Jesus came into the world, she said, solely through "God who created him and woman who bore him." "Man," she asks, "where is your part?" In that one sentence, she overturned the patriarchal, theological tradition she was heir to, one based on the passing of divine power from a heavenly father to a savior son. She saw a woman's birthing as cosmically significant. If gestational language had been key to the "world-making and world-breaking capacities of racial slavery," as Hartman argues, here we see a variation on that gestational language being used by a former slave for liberatory purposes. Truth appropriates her oppressor's tools, perhaps. Or maybe the language about birth was simply hers; she spoke out of experiences defined so significantly by birth, loss, and love that they gave her access to original views about the order of creation, the inescapable place of birth in human life, and the creative, world-making potential of birthing women.

The difficulty in arguing this point, of course, is that every word of Truth's that comes down to us was filtered through the lens of someone else's language. Her most famous words seem unlikely to have been hers, and they misrepresent what appears to have been her experience as a birthing mother. "I have borne thirteen chillen, and seen 'em mos' all sold off into slavery, and when I cried out with a mother's grief, none but Jesus heard—and ar'n't I a woman?" This is the most famous line from the speech at the Akron women's convention, but it was attributed to her only twelve years later, by Frances Dana Gage, a white abolitionist and feminist. It does not appear in Marius Robinson's account. Why did her five real children become thirteen? Did she actually say this, or is this Frances Dana Gage rehearsing a racist stereotype, turning a black woman into a pro-creative machine? Or was Gage just caught in her own experience as a self-made, working-class mother of eight, a woman who at the time had no rights to property, her own earned income, or the children she had birthed? Like Mary Wollstonecraft, Gage was an early feminist who strongly stressed the bodily strength of poor, laboring women, seeing in that strength agency and the potential for action.

o o o

Women's procreative, bodily strength was both an oppressive stereotype and a liberatory resource for early members of the women's movement. Another famous account of Truth relates to a "breast-baring incident" that occurred after a speech she made in 1858 in Indiana. After she spoke, a pro-slavery group of men accused her of being a man and challenged her to bare her breast to the women in the audience, to give bodily proof of her womanhood. Truth reportedly didn't hesitate; without any sense of shame, she bared her breast to her audience and "told them that her breasts had suckled many a white babe . . . that some of those white babies had grown to man's estate." Those white babies who had suckled her colored breasts were, she told them, more manly than her accusers. She disrobed not to her shame, but to their shame. As she disrobed, she asked them if they too wanted to suck.

The quickness of her biting wit is on full display here, her ingeniousness in turning her objectification into these men's infantilization. Women's sexuality—"the madonna–whore imagery of the bare human breast"—is a source of natal power, one that all of humanity has depended upon for its very existence. We were all once suckling children, at the mercy of a woman's strength, love, and care. "Her skillful remaking employed the all-too-common exhibition of an undressed black body," her biographer Nell Irvin Painter writes, "with its resonance of the slave auction that undressed women for sale. What had been intended as degradation became a triumph of embodied rhetoric."

Was Truth merely playing into another stereotype: the mammy, the large-breasted, black, nurturing, witty, asexual woman who takes care of other people's children and seems patiently and humorously accepting of her inferior status? Or were these stereotypes so embedded in the minds of the literate people who recorded her talks that they distorted her words? The layers of representation and self-representation are hard to separate. She's discoverable only through the refracted glass of other people's experiences. It must also be remembered that she was dictating and speaking largely to and for white audiences, and that shaped what she said, what she didn't say, and her narrative emphasis. As Toni Morrison has noted, slave narratives were expected to follow a particular arc. "They created an upbeat story," Morrison explained, one that roughly goes: "I was born, it was terrible, I got out, and other people are still there and you should help them get out."

But perhaps the suspicion some might have that Truth's belief in nurture and her celebration of a mother's body are merely evidence of her oppression is wrong. Why is it so hard to believe that a woman who has been through enormous suffering and has lost many of the people dearest to her would consider nurture vital to any just and flourishing society? It makes sense that Truth would indict the dominant culture not for the saccharine maternal stereotypes it held, but first and foremost for its inability to see the mother figure and the life and sustenance she gives to other people as important. Freedom without care would be disastrous. The problem for her wasn't just that black women had performed laborious caretaking roles, but that white women and men had spurned them. Her assertion of her maternity, furthermore, wouldn't have been understood as a reinforcement of norms; it was a radical claiming of what she had been denied. A slave woman, again, wasn't considered a mother. In slavery, birthing and maternity were split apart.

Truth's speeches resonate strongly with Mary Wollstonecraft's writings (and with Mary Shelley's, to a lesser degree), and they both challenge twenty-first-century paradigms about birth and maternity. What they both seemed to understand is that someone needs to do the nurturing. A culture that turns away from its own children, believing that someone else should feed them and that parental or domestic servility is an insult to one's freedom, is a society that will have to rely on the servile labor provided by a different group of people. Nurture itself wasn't the problem; the problem was that the responsibility to nurture wasn't equally shared by the members of society, and that nurture wasn't given a role in the project of cultural renewal. By the twentieth and twenty-first centuries, many prominent black feminists would make similar arguments. These arguments often come as a surprise to those who see black motherhood as an intrinsically oppressive state.

Labor, humanity, family, women, love, care: these were all

themes repeated by Sojourner Truth as she traveled and preached. The nineteenth century, again, was a time when sickly, dying women were idolized, but Truth eschewed sickness and death and turned her attention toward life. In her last decades, she was often described as dying, as old and near death. But she lived on, passing away in the morning of November 26, 1883, at about the age of eighty-six. During that time, people also testified to her "vital spark" and "life forces," her "indomitable courage fanned to an undying flame," and her "fervor" and "enthusiasm." Olive Gilbert wrote that "her religion is not tinctured in the least with gloom. No doubt, no hesitation, no despondency, spreads a cloud over her soul; but all is bright, clear, positive, and at times ecstatic."

As she traveled and preached, she carried a book with her and filled it with the signatures of the people she met. She called it her Book of Life. That Book of Life was not just a record of her individual life; it was a testament to her encounters with other people, and it is full of the promise of the more just world they were collectively trying to create. Her friend Frances W. Titus would publish her own version of this Book of Life, a fragmentary account of Truth's life as she remembered it but also as it had been recorded by others in various letters, records, and published articles. In that *Book of Life*, Titus tells us that Truth abhorred the past, with its whips and auction blocks, and she grieved for all suffering in the present. But she also "peered toward the future with sibyl eyes, her heart beat loud and fast; for she saw in it all grand possibilities." If only the voice of maternity would be heard, she believed, then the welfare of all generations, both present and future, would be assured.

In one of her last speeches, in 1880, when she was well into her eighties, she spoke not of endings but of beginnings. These beginnings were defined very differently from how they were for Hannah

Arendt. "We talk of a beginning, but there is no beginning but the beginning of a wrong. All else is from God, and is from everlasting to everlasting." Still, that sense of everlastingness did not refute the possibilities of change and renewal. There, on the brink of her own death, witnessing the failures of Reconstruction and the sputtering progress of the campaign for women's rights, she said defiantly, as if the speaking might bring it into being: "This has become a new world."

—6—

The Will to Change

American poet and critic Adrienne Rich was born on May 16, 1929, in Baltimore, Maryland. That was the year Virginia Woolf's *A Room of One's Own* was first published in London and around the time Hannah Arendt met her first husband in Germany, soon after her breakup with Martin Heidegger and a few months before the stock market crash of 1929. Arendt was old enough to be Rich's mother, a fact I constantly reminded myself of as I read them side by side, learning from and comparing their different versions of natality, ideas shaped by their distinct if overlapping life experiences. They both inhabited New York's literary circles in the middle of the twentieth century, and they both saw birth as an integral and underdeveloped part of our human story, a counterweight to nihilism, and a catalyst for political change. Action, revolution, poetry, politics, freedom, tradition, history, power, race, democracy, and change—both women focused on these themes as they simultaneously developed two of the richest and most expansive twentieth-century accounts of birth.

But they developed their ideas about birth on parallel tracks, rarely meeting. In the 1970s, Rich, by then a converted radical feminist, turned to Arendt's *The Human Condition* excitedly, eager to hear what a major political philosopher and highly respected woman intellectual had to say about the question of women and work. She was greatly disappointed. In a scathing review, she called it a "lofty and crippled book," one that showcased the "tragedy of a female mind nourished on male ideology." Gender was at the heart of Rich's critique of Arendt's work. Where Arendt had erred, she believed, was in developing her theories about birth without also paying close attention to women's bodies and the labor they perform, often without recognition. "The personal is political," Rich, like other second wave feminists, believed, but this was a slogan that Arendt's work implicitly dismissed. Politics was, for Arendt, where we step out from our personal and private lives, from our individual homes and the labor we perform there, and where we embark on the project of our plural existence.

Many of the women in Rich's generation felt bound within those homes. That is where they gave birth to and raised their children. Their political understanding of birth would stay closely connected with women's bodies and the labor they performed behind what many of them described as closed doors.

o o o

Adrienne Rich's father, Arnold Rice Rich, was the son of a secular Jewish refugee from Kassa, Hungary, who had founded a successful shoe store. He grew up in the confident, steady stream of upward mobility, scoring professional successes as he became a highly regarded pathologist. Around the time Hannah Arendt was born, he was enrolled in a Virginia military academy, being shaped by a military training that his parents hoped would help with his assimilation, would mold him into a Southern gentleman, one destined for American greatness.

Arnold Rich went on to study medicine, and after a decade-long courtship, he married Helen Jones, a Gentile woman, an Episcopalian—a Southern WASP and an aspiring musician—born in Wilmington, North Carolina, in 1893. Rich would think back through both of her parents as she grew up and became a poet, but she'd also look deeper into her personal history, to the women who had birthed her parents: her grandmothers, Mary Gravely and Hattie Rice, whose late-nineteenth-century-lives, she wrote, "I begin to imagine."

Rich's maternal grandmother, Mary Gravely, was a literate woman, educated at a convent as a child, and she aspired to be a poet and playwright but ended up married to a "jovial alcoholic," from whom she eventually separated. Needing to support three children, she worked as a real estate agent in New York City, and her creative career never took off. But her poetic interests and achievements would not go unnoticed by her granddaughter, nor would her grief. One poem Mary Gravely published in 1909, when she was already a mother, spoke to what would have been a private, incalculable loss. She titled it "To a Still-Born Babe."

Rich's mother, daughter of this jovial alcoholic who recklessly and amiably squandered the family's money and this literate, independent, grieving woman, would be a strangely absent figure for Rich throughout her life, although she lived long into her old age, dying at one hundred and two. Her mother lived in Rich's background, maintaining for Rich a stillborn quality. Rich's recent biographer Hilary Holladay calls Helen Jones Rich "opaquely smiling," a "faint star whose vague outline never came into focus." And Rich herself grew up feeling that her birth had sent her mother into a narcotic coma from which she never awoke.

Rich would later critique her mother's slavish obedience to a patriarchal script about women's roles as wives and mothers—a slavishness that ironically resulted not in over-mothering but in a haunting, maternal absence, an inability to shield her daughter from her father's domineering presence or to nurture her daughters out of her own creative womanhood. While Hannah Arendt had grown up around women after her father's early death and maintained a strong relationship with her mother until her mother's death, Rich's prevailing parental presence was that of her father, one whose dominion was lorded over her from the time she was in the womb. Arnold Rice saw women's bodies as impure and disliked the way they smelled. He found pregnant women ugly, and he forced his wife to remain inactive and hidden while baby Adrienne gestated in her womb. For him, a pure woman was white and bloodless, a "gardenia blanched by moonlight, staining around the edges when touched." Arnold Rich averted his gaze from his pregnant wife, as if to not see what was happening.

Baby Adrienne, the couple's first child, was born after a long, slow, painful labor that months of inactivity may have exacerbated. She'd later write that she was "born in my father's workplace, a hospital in the Black ghetto, whose lobby contained an immense white marble statue of Christ." Arnold could not name the baby after himself because of her gender, but he bequeathed to her his "A" and his sister's middle name. In a letter written days after her birth, Arnold boasted that his daughter was born multilingual. She would be his project, his little prodigy, stamped from birth by his family name and born into his place of employment. He was a doctor, an authority who understood the mysteries of the human body in ways that his obedient, piano-playing wife could not.

Rich's father would overtake her mother in her childhood memories, but from her earliest years she recalled her mother's sensuous, feminine body and a love between them that was "subliminal, subversive, preverbal," based on "the knowledge flowing between two alike bodies, one of which has spent nine months inside the other." Her mother's bodily presence reverberated through her life, beginning with the pregnancy and the postnatal period, shaping her own consciousness, and working as a lifelong matrilineal bequest. Her mother, once a successful musician, had sacrificed her own creative life and unusual talents to take care of her child and her husband, a fact which gradually drove mother and daughter apart.

When Rich was about four, she experienced a seismic rupture, which she'd later describe as the loss of her own little Garden of Eden. When her sister was born, her mother's attention was stolen from her and she was left primarily to her father's care. As her mother was consumed with caring for the baby, Rich's father began teaching his first daughter to read. These developments resulted in what felt to Rich like a change in lineage; she moved from the mother-line to the father-line, coming entirely under her father's charismatic and tyrannical power, a power he maintained through language.

She strove to faithfully fulfill her father's dreams. His dreams were her dreams. They shared them. She was a young wunderkind, learning to read and write at age four and publishing her first volume of poetry at age six with his assistance. She gradually left behind her childhood training as a pianist, which her mother had nurtured. Over eight decades spanning two centuries, she never turned from her vocation as a poet, but she turned from her father, later describing him and his parenting style as "egotistical, tyrannical, opinionated, and terribly wearing." Her mother, meanwhile, offered no buffer; Rich felt that she had enabled Arnold's dominion, that she had willingly sacrificed her daughter to her husband. The young Rich threw sporadic tantrums, but also obediently complied, applying herself to her work with an uncanny confidence and discipline. But a neither–nor sense of self haunted her. She didn't feel like the girl everyone expected her to be. Sometimes she didn't feel like a girl at all.

Rich thought about birth from a young age, sensing in it a great center of human power, sacredness, and mystery. Her father had an obstetrics textbook in his study, written by the doctor who had delivered her, and from its pages she learned about the perineum, episiotomies, and crowning heads. Looking at the photos of fragmented body parts, she feared her body would never withstand such a "cataclysm." Rich's mother spoke to her about sex and conception with an unusual candor for a woman of that era, but labor remained a mystery. Rich turned to literature and by the age of twelve, she was obsessively reading and rereading the passages in novels by Leo Tolstoy and Pearl Buck that depicted birth. She intuited that birth was a great transformation, a move from the familiar to the strange, and she was drawn to its fecundity. But birth—like her mother—felt elusive. It's as if she was trying to read her way to a mother she still needed and felt abandoned by, to wake them both in the recognition of birth's power, and to thereby repair the broken links in her maternal lineage. But that rupture would prove impossible to repair.

o o o

Hannah Arendt and Adrienne Rich were both connected by and distinguished by their Jewishness. Arendt, again, understood herself as ineradicably Jewish by birth. Rich, in contrast, was split at the root by birth as the daughter of a white Southern Protestant woman and a Jewish son of immigrants. She wrote, "If it is true that 'we think back through our mothers if we are women' (Virginia Woolf)— and I myself have affirmed this—then . . . I cannot (or need not?)

count myself a Jew." But she was by blood half Jewish. This made her, according to the Nazis, of mixed blood and thereby "nonexempt from the Final Solution." She'd realize to her dawning horror that her half-WASP pedigree would not have saved her in Nazi Germany. And eventually, she would drift back to her ancestral faith, identifying as a secular Jew.

Her father always downplayed his Jewishness. His family had changed their name to hide their Jewish roots, and while he pored over the Old Testament in his study, he didn't identify with the Jewish people culturally or religiously. Decades later, she'd understand how his medical career had likely been stalled by anti-Semitism, although she never heard him complain of discrimination. She'd eventually grasp the price of the prejudices he encountered with more sympathy, the vulnerability his tyrannical manner must have masked, but that silence and those erasures impoverished her, she lamented, warping her trajectory, and she'd find them hard to forgive.

The erasures were particularly egregious because of when they occurred. As Rich was learning to read and losing her connection with her mother, Hitler came to power. The Nazis' extermination of the Jews was devastating Europe as she was busy perfecting her poetic craft in her pressure cooker of a family, but she grew up unaware of the Holocaust and virtually unaware of World War II, which her country entered when she was twelve. It was over when she turned sixteen, and she wondered if the war's end might return her to the more weightless concerns of an average American teenage girl: lipstick, nylons, boys.

Around this time, however, she started independently reading about the concentration camps in the newspaper. Alone, she trekked to a local theater in Baltimore and viewed footage of the Allies liberating the camps. Her viewing birthed a horrible realization: "every one of those piles of corpses, mountains of shoes and clothing had contained, simply, individuals, who had believed, as I now believed of myself, that they were intended to live out a life of some kind of meaning, that the world possessed some kind of sense and order; yet *this* had happened to them." She realized she was connected to the dead by a deep taboo—Jewishness, her "messy, noisy, unpredictable, maybe poor" biological ancestry, even as she had grown up under the cover of her mother's WASP, Gentile order, singing Christian hymns and getting baptized into a Protestant church whose catechism she never believed in. Sitting in that theater, she had a fleeting dream of traveling to Europe as a journalist and "recording the rebirth of civilization after the fall of the Nazis." Like Hannah Arendt, she was convinced that Europe would need to be reborn.

But when she came home from the theater and described what she had seen, her parents were not impressed by her awakening, her newfound knowledge of current events, or her budding compassion for the victims of genocide. She was scolded for her morbidity, for sniffing around for death. She was folded back into the family's antebellum mansion, a beautiful brick house on a hill accented with white columns and surrounded by trees in an upscale Baltimore neighborhood, a planned suburb with a history of anti-Semitism and anti-black policies. It was a privileged life but also a profoundly withdrawn one, cut off from the rest of the world and propelled by its own internally eddying intensities.

Rich's sense of natality would grow out of such morbidities: the piles of corpses, the shunned selves, the taboo identities, the lost mothers, the unutterable words. She would also wrestle with the history of such houses, with how our experience and understanding of birth is shaped by private property, by the histories of nuclear families enclosed in their separate, walled-off spaces, by their restrictive inwardness, by the loneliness of the women who labored there, often exhausted and largely unrecognized for their unpaid labor, and by the fraught, alive world that existed just outside their deadening echo chambers.

o o o

Adrienne Rich left Baltimore for Cambridge, Massachusetts, in 1947, enrolling in Radcliffe College, where she excelled academically, wore high heels and stockings, effectively navigated the neighboring male world of Harvard, and dated boys. While still an undergraduate, she got engaged, describing marriage as heavenly and proclaiming that she wanted four children—three sons and one daughter. These family plans ran parallel to professional aspirations, their lateral tracks running off into an impeccable future. She had just won the prestigious Yale Series of Younger Poets Prize after her manuscript was chosen by W. H. Auden in 1950, a remarkable coup for someone of her age and gender. A bright poetic career and a fulfilling family life lay before her, harmonizing in her imagination. Her first mature book would be published in 1951 as *A Change of World*, titled after a minor poem in the collection but picking up on a theme that would define her life and work: change. "What new shapes," she asked, "will be worn next year"?

The world was indeed changing, but not always in ways that Rich, despite her prophetic instincts, could clearly foresee. In the 1950s America was at the height of its international power, expanding politically, economically, and culturally, cresting on propitious waves of postwar optimism that weren't, regrettably, shared by all Americans. Between 1950 and 1973, around the time Rich published her most celebrated poetry collection, *Diving into the Wreck*, the global economy expanded at the fastest pace ever recorded. The university system ballooned, more books were published than ever before, and American culture spread across the globe. Most Western countries experienced historically low levels of inequality and political opposition as a robust middle class thrived. Despite Cold War tensions and the persistence of racial segregation, a widespread belief in the resilient promise of democracy still inspired many people. Many Westerners trusted their leaders and their political and cultural institutions. The free world had defeated Nazism and would defend the world from other totalitarian regimes.

But the 1950s were also notorious as a stifling period for women. As men came back from war, they resumed the jobs that women had filled in their absence. An ideological backlash against feminism's first wave compounded women's economic and professional setbacks and, by most measures, women were worse off by the end of the decade than they were at its beginning. Increasing wealth made possible a migration to the suburbs for many families. Outside the cities, families went nuclear, surrounded by white picket fences, living in roomy houses that weren't always as idyllic as they looked. Women began marrying and giving birth earlier than their parents had, and they had more children. The baby boom flourished, a result of buoyant optimism and economic vitality, but also of a regressive ideology that wanted to keep women at home, away from public and professional spaces.

Rich was part of a "silent generation" of women whose lives were thwarted by what Betty Friedan called "the feminine mystique," the myth of homemaking and childbearing as women's highest calling. Some members of this silent generation, including Rich, would not stay silent for long; they'd go on to spearhead second-wave feminism and participate in the various social justice movements in the second half of the century. For Rich, who had been writing poetry since childhood and who had had her voice strongly affirmed, a rejection of the feminine mystique would mean more than eschewing silence and returning to writing and poetry readings after her first pregnancy. It would demand a much more fundamental and challenging task: the reinvention of language itself. What language would allow for female lineages, tender and loving relationships between women across generations, and what words—what troubled, more honest syntax—could help her reimagine her society, to make women's daily creative lives more central to its politics and culture?

But she wasn't quite there yet. At the age of twenty-four, with a string of early poetic successes, she married Alfred Conrad, a Harvard economics professor, a Jewish man her father disapproved of. Rich broke away from her father and replaced him with another largely assimilated, Jewish, high-achieving male figure. She became pregnant with her first child after her second book was accepted for publication by a major publisher. Though she should have been encouraged by this professional milestone, she stopped writing and reading anything of substance, drifting toward housekeeping magazines and childcare books while pregnant. Reinforcing this retreat from her intellectual pursuits, a poetry reading she was supposed to give at a New England boys' prep school was canceled after the headmaster heard she was seven months along. The boys, he feared, wouldn't be able to listen to her poetry when they saw she was carrying a baby.

She understood that the world suddenly perceived her only as a pregnant woman and being exclusively a pregnant body felt easier to her at this juncture. It was a strange relief from her intellectual ambitions. But her body revolted. Two days before giving birth to a son, she broke out in what was first diagnosed as measles but later explained as an allergic reaction to the pregnancy. She felt alienated from her body, which she handed over to her male doctors to procure the birth of her child. She had been raised to see birth as a passive experience and, on the verge of giving birth, she assumed the role of passive vessel. The goal was motherhood; labor and delivery were only painful, fearful experiences to be obliviously endured.

At the time of her first child's birth, she was a fresh bride, a dutiful daughter, and a highly literate and ambitious reader of housekeeping magazines. What she didn't know was that she was about to be radicalized. The experience that would radicalize her was not the civil rights movement or the women's movement or any other movement at all. It was childbirth.

o o o

David, her first son, was born on March 28, 1955, under general anesthesia. Coincidentally, he was born on Rich's father's birthday. She had given birth to the son everyone wanted, including her, but in the postnatal period she felt oddly deflated. She'd later claim that what she more urgently needed and wanted at that time was "to give birth, at twenty-five, to my unborn self, the self that our father-centered family had suppressed in me." Looking back at her unconsciousness and passivity, she'd see herself as essentially still a nineteenth-century woman as far as birth was concerned. But that was all about to change.

After her son was born, she was catastrophically exhausted, worn out by the constant, fragmented tedium, and she struggled to write. In her own silence, she felt a growing, gnawing desire: to remake her life. But the incessant demands of childcare bound her to the home where she was expected to be the "Victorian Lady of Leisure, the Angel in the House, and also the Victorian cook, scullery maid, laundress, governess, and nurse." The Victorian Age may have long passed, but the specter of Victorian domesticity still haunted her and other women of her race and class. She was unproductive, restless, angry, and depressed, but at the same time she was in love with her son and amazed by his newborn being. She found herself profoundly conflicted, living "at the deepest levels of passion and confusion."

Soon enough, she was pregnant again. A second son, Paul (nicknamed Pablo), was born on July 17, 1957, again under general anesthesia, and he was delivered by the same obstetrician. By the following summer, she was pregnant for the third time. While her résumé is full of professional successes from these years, she worried about and lamented her own poetic fallowness. She started reading Simone de Beauvoir, imagining new possibilities. When she met Sylvia Plath during her third pregnancy, she strongly advised her fellow poet not to have children. She had resolved that this child would be her last; she would be sterilized after the delivery.

That resolution worked like a strange conversion, giving her a new sense of control over her procreative life but simultaneously allowing her to accept that third pregnancy and birth with a greater sense of openness to its difficulty. On one level, she didn't want another child, but she wouldn't consider an abortion, she decided; she welcomed the birth of that third child with an "affirming fatalism," sensing in his unborn being an inevitability, a life she must bring to bear "as an additional weapon against drift, stagnation and spiritual death." She wasn't sleepwalking anymore. She saw her whole life up until this point as a struggle to give birth, in life and in art, to a new creation. What she feared most was death, and even in her exhaustion and despair, she felt that these pregnancies and parturitions were also giving birth to her. Birth radicalized her, brought her down to her root, the source of her being. This drilling down into her own stratified bedrock may have been internal work, but it would make her an activist, one invested in the political, cultural, and social transformation of society.

On March 4, 1959, she gave birth again under general anesthesia to her third and youngest son, Jacob. Twenty-four hours after giving birth, she woke up as a new person: the mother of three boys and a sterilized woman. "Had yourself spayed, did you?" her nurse asked her as she woke from the anesthetic. To be granted that sterilization, she had had to petition a committee of physicians in a letter signed by her husband, presenting her justification for the operation. Many American women were being coerced into sterilizations at this time, but as a white middle-to-upper-class woman, she had not been seen as a prime candidate for sterilization. She had to argue her case. She already had three children, she explained, and she suffered from rheumatoid arthritis, which had been diagnosed when she was twenty-two. This appears to have convinced the committee to grant her request. Thus began a new chapter of her life, one in which she readily admitted to a friend that she was not born to be a mother. She recommitted herself to poetry, which became a refuge from motherhood, a place where she could live as no one's mother.

She was an impatient mother, she confessed. She felt that the demands of caring for her sons were eating away at her, stymieing her, but at the same time she passionately loved those three small bodies, which astounded her with their "beauty, humor, and physical affection." She saw them not as the heirs of patriarchy but as the "sweet flesh of infants, the delicate insistency of exploring bodies, the purity of concentration, grief, or joy which exists undiluted in young children" and which opened her up to "long forgotten zones in myself."

In one exquisite passage, she describes the "delicious" rhythm she experienced with her sons one summer in Vermont when their father was away for work. She discarded routines and rules and, over a relaxed series of hot, clear days, they ate outdoors, "hand-to-mouth":

> We lived half-naked, stayed up to watch bats and stars and fire-flies, read and told stories, slept late. I watched their slender little-boys' bodies grow brown, we washed in warm water from the garden hose lying in the sun, we lived like castaways on some island of mothers and children. At night they fell asleep without murmur and I stayed up reading and writing as I had when a student, till the early morning hours.

Driving home, she felt elated, believing she had glimpsed a new possibility: a motherhood, a relationship between her body and the bodies she had birthed, that was not defined by what she had resisted, by what she would eventually call "the institution of motherhood." She and her sons were coconspirators, outlaws from that institution, and she briefly felt in charge of her life.

o o o

In the years after her sons were born, Rich transformed herself, experiencing the 1960s in New York City, participating in the civil rights movement, and becoming a self-described radical feminist. But by 1970, she was in turmoil. Her sons were growing into young men and her husband was retreating emotionally, becoming unreachable. One day she stood at the top of the subway stairs and could not descend. Terrified by her paralysis, she realized she'd need to go further, to change her life more drastically.

Shortly after this incident, she informed her husband that she was renting her own apartment and that the boys would stay with him. She wasn't leaving them, she explained, but she desperately needed space. She moved out and breathed in a new atmosphere. In a letter to a fellow poet, she described how clean and fresh the city's air seemed. She felt that the world was beginning again. But her husband did not savor the new beginning her move had birthed for them. He was convinced she'd lost her mind and he sank into a deep depression. Several weeks later, he drove up to Vermont and fatally shot himself in a meadow where the young family had once happily picnicked. Rich was shocked, angry, scared, devastated. It must have felt like whiplash. In a matter of weeks, she had gone from liberated woman, living on her own, to widowed single mother of three adolescent boys. Several weeks later, her book *The Will to Change* came out. "What does not change," the epigraph of her book reads, quoting American poet Charles Olson, "is the will to change." Amid all devastations, this would remain true for her.

The wound caused by Alfred Conrad's suicide never healed. Decades later, Rich would angrily snap if it was brought up by an interviewer and refuse to discuss it. But she was a survivor, unreservedly committed to life. The "ribs of the disaster" had a "threadbare beauty," she confessed in her most celebrated book, *Diving into the Wreck*, a collection of poems written in 1971 and 1972, in the wake of Alfred's suicide. She had come to see that wreck, equipped only with language, to witness "the damage that was done / and the treasures that prevail." The treasure that prevailed was life itself. In "From a Survivor," she wrote of her husband, now wastefully dead, and of how he'd never make the "leap" they had once dreamed of making together, perhaps into their mutually livable future. Without him now, the leap was no longer a leap but a "succession of brief, amazing movements / each one making possible the next." Her husband's death would radically alter her course, painfully ending a chapter of her life, but it would not destroy her.

In subsequent years, she came out as a lesbian and committed herself to the feminist movement, a movement that she described as passionately and erotically charged. Through various relationships, jobs, and moves, she raised her sons haphazardly and tenderly as a single mother who made a living from poetry, essays, and teaching. She never stopped writing, and in looking at the body of work she left behind, one sees indeed a succession of brief, amazing movements, each one pregnant with some tenacious, natal seed.

o o o

Seventeen years after the birth of her last son and six years after her husband's suicide, she published *Of Woman Born: Motherhood as Experience and Institution*, one of the most ambitious and significant twentieth-century prose accounts of birth and motherhood in the English language. First published in 1976, it soon became a touchstone for many of the books on birth and motherhood that came after it, and it remains a key text for many feminists today.

Before it came out, pioneering feminists like Simone de Beauvoir and Shulamith Firestone had argued that maternity was the root of women's oppression. Rich didn't deny this oppression in *Of Woman Born*, but she argued that birth was simultaneously the root of women's power. Motherhood, she agreed, was the site at which female potentialities throughout history had been literally "massacred." But the book is also a constructive manifesto arguing for the active, affirmative, imaginative, and transformative power that she saw in birth, one that subverted the "deep, fatalistic pessimism as to the possibilities of change" that she found in many male poets. She saw within birth the relational, fertile energy of creation itself—"the very plenitude of creation, the exhilarating variance of nature." "Every infant born," she wrote, "is testimony to the intricacy and breadth of possibilities inherent in humanity."

It's a book she was only ready to write when she felt unambivalent enough in her love for her children to explore birth's painful, incomprehensible, and ambiguous territory—"a ground hedged by taboos, mined with false-namings" but also characterized by passionate love, delight, and amazement. She resisted its domestication, but motherhood, she believed, had been "fulfilling even in its sorrows, a key to the meaning of life."

The book has endured for its trenchant critique and the depth of its research, its tremendous range and inclusive ambition, but also because of its irreducibility to one register; Rich captures the complex paradoxes of birth and motherhood not with a flattened, cool, or diffident ambivalence, but with a passionate exhilaration and desperate sense of degradation. Her most sweeping goal was not to free women from the demands of other people (although sometimes a relief from such demands was required) but to grant women the license to direct their creative energies outward at the world, not just inward to the nuclear family. She wanted to derive from women's procreative bodies and from birth more radical social, cultural, and political implications.

Rich was critiquing a distinct variety of motherhood: one particular to women of her race, class, and nationality, a motherhood that was not some innate aspect of the human condition but a particular institution with a specific history and ideology. This institutional motherhood had grown up alongside capitalism and its beneficiaries, the more prosperous members of Western societies. With industrialization, work had moved outside the home, and roles had become more starkly defined along gender lines, with motherhood becoming a full-time, exclusive vocation tied to the home for women in families that could rely on one spouse's income. Home, she argued, had become a place to retreat from the world, an ideal realm infused with sacred meanings. A working mother became a creature distinct from a stay-at-home mother, and she was often criticized for her moral neglect of her family. The stay-at-home mother, in turn, didn't always experience her home as a safe and cozy retreat. In the privacy of their homes, women became more isolated from one another and from their spouses; fathers grew estranged from the daily lives of women and children. In the 1950s, with the explosion of the suburbs, the real estate market became a key engine of wealth creation and things got worse. In 1986, when a revised edition of *Of Woman Born* came out, houses were being built bigger and bigger in wealthy pockets around the globe, with advanced security systems marketed to their fearful inhabitants, but marital rape was still not a criminal offense in twenty-one American states and Americans were stockpiling guns. Was a woman safe at home?

Patriarchy, Rich argued, is based on the idea of family as a unit of possession. Family is often presented as the building block of society, but she believed that it could also work as a negation of the world we share in common with other people. The family, as a unit, could be individualistic and competitive with other families, rather than cooperative. For much of the written history that she was heir to, families were hierarchically structured, and a man's family was his property. Like whatever wealth he created, it would outlive him; his children, particularly his sons, would provide a means of surviving his own death through the transmission of his genes, his name, his legacy, and his inheritance. The concept of motherhood Rich was trying to dismantle had developed at "this crossroads of sexual possession, property ownership, and the desire to transcend death." As a mother, she had chafed at the inwardness, her inability to leave her home or see another person for days—the tight, suffocating circle that enclosed her and her children and denied them contact with a larger world. But liberation wasn't just a matter of leaving the home, or of building a career.

In her bestselling 1963 book *The Feminine Mystique*, Betty Friedan had, again, given a name to this disparate set of problems and symptoms, ones unique to a generation of women, largely white and from middle-class or more privileged backgrounds, women who had married young and had large numbers of children in the context of a booming economy. They had their lovely, enviable homes, their appliances—vacuum cleaners, toasters, refrigerators—and few economic demands placed upon them. And yet they were bored, tired, and dissatisfied; they felt like mere props for their husbands, like thankless servants to their children. The highlight of their day was cocktail hour when their husbands came home and they would drink. Their complaints have been critiqued as self-centered, oblivious, spoiled, and "whiny," and they can appear self-indulgent in comparison, for instance, to the life of Sojourner Truth, or to the forced sterilizations and abortions that were denying motherhood to many non-white, poor, and disabled women around the globe.

The problem wasn't the demands of motherhood or domesticity, Friedan argued, or any lack of privilege. As wealth and privilege increased, she thought, the situation actually got worse. It was the passivity and loneliness of it all. It was the way motherhood and marriage had been paired with consumption, isolation, private property, and gadgets.

Like Friedan and other second-wave feminists, Rich was seeking women's liberation and empowerment not just in the political realm but in the domestic one as well. But she went further than Friedan in imagining the potential for radical, societal change. She dug deep into history, looking for civilizational models which had women, birth, and maternity at their center. With an omnivorous, zealous curiosity, she unearthed accounts of ancient pre-patriarchal, matriarchal, or gynarchic communities that worshipped mother goddesses and recognized a tremendous, unrivaled power implicit in women's bodies: the power of creation, the potential to create and sustain life itself. Sometimes this power was put toward birthing new human lives; at other times it was put toward creating other things, such as earthen pottery. Rich dug up these examples, archaeological or anthropological, not for the sake of establishing any historical fact but for the sake of birthing a new imaginary, one in which women weren't secondary creatures and birth was more power than passivity. What would society look like if birth was understood not as the site of women's oppression but as the source of humanity's creative, active being? What had been lost when earth gods became sun gods like Apollo—rational, bright, highly ordered deities stripped of their irrational, darker female attributes, which were dumped on Dionysus, Apollo's chaotic underside?

The goal was not to reestablish matriarchy or to imagine a female utopia (although Rich sympathized at times with female separatists), and it certainly wasn't to bolster any pro-natalist beliefs. The potential for transformation lay in how birth breaks down the dualisms humans use to structure reality—the dualisms, again, of man/woman, mind/body, thought/experience, destruction/creation, self/other, creator/created. Birth exposes the ambiguities of our being, our vulnerability and dependence, our pain and subjectivity, but also our potent, creative potential.

o o o

The year *Of Woman Born* was published, Rich wrote her critique of Hannah Arendt's *The Human Condition* in an essay about women's work. The problem she had with the book was not merely that Arendt paid little attention to other women writers, but that she had conceptually slammed the door on women's experiences, particularly on those which related to their bodies. This is the passage from *The Human Condition* that really bothered Rich:

> The daily fight in which the human body is engaged to keep the world clean and prevent its decay bears little resemblance to heroic deeds; the endurance it needs to repair every day anew the waste of yesterday is not courage, and what makes the effort painful is not danger but its relentless repetition.

Rich responded by describing this repetitive work in considerable detail:

> The million tiny stitches, the friction of the scrubbing brush, the scouring cloth, the iron across the shirt, the rubbing of cloth against itself to exorcise the stain, the renewal of the scorched pot, the rusted knifeblade, the invisible weaving of a frayed and threadbare family life, the cleaning up of soil and waste left behind by men and children . . .

Such work, Rich believed, was women's work—a mother's work and a wife's work—and she herself had not particularly enjoyed it. She didn't fetishize it, but she knew that it mattered to society and that it took courage to perform such endless labor day after day. Arendt had not just averted her gaze from the problem of women's labor, Rich argued; she had instead looked straight through it, not seeing women's lives at all. Hers was an old blindness. For millennia women's work had been deemed irrelevant, a mere footnote in the broader story of civilization.

Rich, as a mother of three boys, argued powerfully that the "million tiny stitches" that constitute a mother's incessant daily work, the feeding and cleaning and life-sustaining activities that mothers perform largely behind closed doors, were socially, politically, and culturally crucial. She saw in them the "activity of world-protection, world-preservation, world-repair" that Arendt believed was only possible in other realms. Labor, as Arendt called such work, is not public work and it should be kept hidden. But Rich saw a problem in this logic, believing that Arendt had effectively misappropriated birth, taking it from women and from the burdens of biology, abstracting it and turning a woman's organic being—the very "source of her awe and her original powers"—against her.

Rich was right: women are not at the center of Arendt's work. Arendt was no feminist. Her thinking had been shaped by her schooling in a patriarchal philosophical tradition, but also by the Holocaust, which had brought a different set of concerns to the fore of her consciousness. While Rich had been a high-achieving girl living in a prosperous Baltimore neighborhood, Hannah Arendt had been fleeing Nazi Germany, during her peak childbearing years. While Rich, the wife of a successful academic, had been hiring housekeepers to help her with chores, Arendt had herself been working as a housekeeper, trying to learn English, living as a conscious pariah defined indelibly by her Jewishness. Rich, meanwhile, was an assimilated half-Jew, one whose family had benefited from the disavowal of their Jewish roots, and who consistently sought belonging in her life, not exclusion.

Arendt would have furthermore distrusted Rich's stark demarcation between male minds and female minds, between male and female activities, and not only because of her immersion in writings penned by men. She had witnessed the essentialism of the anti-Semites, and how their rigid categories of people, of enemies and allies, had hardened into ideologies that had warped the minds of millions of people. She'd also borne witness to the systematic slaughter of millions of men, both Jews and non-Jews—men who in the gas chambers had been divested violently of the patriarchal power Rich attributes broadly to the male half of the species. Arendt distanced herself from feminists, refusing to identify strongly as a woman. But Rich's encounter with radical feminism helped her birth herself, drill down deep into her being, and imagine new possibilities for herself and her world.

o o o

The possibility of significant societal and personal change and a wonder at life itself would be the treasure that prevailed in Rich's long, intensely energetic life and in her capacious work, both of which were full of twists and unexpected turns and were challenged by her disability, before her death in 2012. In the last pages of *Of Woman Born*, she imagined a version of women's procreative capacities that wasn't based on models of a wilderness waiting to be exploited or the assembly line, on agricultural fertility goddesses or an immaculate Madonna. If woman could become the presiding genius of her own body, she believed, she would be able to "truly create new life, bringing forth not only children (if and as we choose) but the visions, and the thinking, necessary to sustain, console, and alter human existence—a new relationship to the universe." This is where the possibility of real change came for her: the transformation of thought, based on a deeper and richer understanding of women's lives and their bodies.

Up until her last lectures, Rich was talking about a future that could still be born. Poetry could help us see what had become forbidden: a "forgotten future: a still-uncreated site whose moral architecture is founded not on ownership and dispossession, the subjection of women . . . but on the continuous redefining of freedom." Such a future was constantly being written off, but she could see it coming into view. It remained to be determined and it would ultimately be created by people who had been born. It demanded no more or less than the "will to change," a "wild patience," a grounding in necessity, and a painstaking sewing of those millions of tiny, life-protecting, life-preserving, life-repairing stitches.

—7—

Ancient Properties

"Do you have any future plans?" an interviewer asked American novelist Toni Morrison in 1981. She succinctly responded, "The future for me is always my children."

Her two sons were on the cusp of manhood by then, and her literary career was taking off. Morrison's fourth novel, *Tar Baby*, had just come out and the interview was part of her publisher's publicity push. The book had landed her on the cover of *Newsweek* and had found a place on the *New York Times* bestseller list within a month of publication. Even more successes would follow in the decades ahead, including a Nobel Prize in Literature in 1993, but Morrison would continually hold those successes in the light of a set of values different from those held dear by the literary marketplace. She was thrilled and self-fulfilled by her ability to nurture her own creative career, but that career had been built on a more expansive sense of nurture. We must nurture ourselves and our own creativity, Morrison believed, but we must also nurture one another. The "tar," she explained in that 1981 interview, was a quality the women she had grown up with had

had: the "ability to hold something together that otherwise would fall apart." It was their nurturing abilities, their "ancient properties," as she called them—their ability to be both "a ship and a safe harbor," to be daughters *and* mothers, accommodating women *and* independent women, women with a home life *and* women with careers.

Tar Baby came out just after Ronald Reagan was elected president. He had come into office espousing "family values"—values undermined, many feared, by women's participation in the workforce. America's female workforce had more than doubled since Morrison's birth, and many saw women's employment as a source of cultural disintegration, believing that family and work were in intrinsic conflict. But Morrison saw no conflict. The black women she had descended from had always had to work, even while raising families, running households, and playing active roles in their communities. These women's examples had fed her, morally and creatively, as a mother and as a writer, and she believed that they must be kept alive. She had her own family values, values based more on the idea of an extended family than a nuclear family. Just as her sons were her future, her ancestors were her past. "If you kill the ancestors, you've just killed everything," she explained. "It's part of the whole nurturing thing."

In remembering her ancestors and in nurturing her sons, she was the tar, holding together not just her family line but time itself. Time, an entirely human concept, unfolds through human births, she believed. Time unfurls back through family lineages, and forward through the lives of children toward a horizon we can only hope for, only imagine. Human birth, in her account, connects us; it is part of what makes us whole beings, integrated into time itself. But that birth is no easy integration. She would depict birth under the most difficult and morally compromised circumstances, putting birth to some of its severest tests in the history of the written word.

Morrison's entire oeuvre is framed by birth; her first novel (*The Bluest Eye*) begins with a pregnancy and her last novel (*God Help the Child*) ends with one. Her imagination is the tar that holds those births together, linking the early-twentieth-century communities she was born into with those born into the twenty-first century and beyond.

"What you do to children matters," a character says in *God Help the Child*. "And they might never forget it." Her work and her life were animated by this conviction.

o o o

Toni Morrison was born Chloe Ardelia Wofford on February 18, 1931, in Lorain, Ohio, a working-class town located about twenty-five miles west of Cleveland. The name her parents gave her came from the Bible, though Chloe is also another name for the Greek goddess of fertility, Demeter. Morrison was born into the American Midwest in the middle of the Great Depression. Lorain was a small town of immigrants from Europe and Mexico, and of American blacks who had largely migrated from the South, seeking better opportunities. Everyone in that mixed-race town was, in her recollections, very poor. She was the second child born to George Wofford, a shipyard welder, and Ella Ramah Wofford, a homemaker who also worked various jobs over the years to help support her family. Throughout her life, Morrison spoke of the warmth of the family she had been raised in, the ways her parents had protected and affirmed her life from her earliest days.

Her mother gave birth to her at home at 2245 Elyria Avenue, in a house that is always mentioned as Morrison's childhood home, although she moved numerous times within Lorain. It was, in any event, her birthplace. "That's my house," she said in a documentary about her life made decades later. Pointing at a series of photographs of a modest, two-story house with a front porch, surrounded by green grass, she said, "That's where I was born, up there in the attic." The attic was very cold, her mother had told her, narrating her own birth to her as she grew up. Hospital births were for "hookers" at that time, she explained. "Married women had their babies at home."

Her father worked at the U.S. Steel factory in town, often holding two other jobs at the same time to support his family. He was afraid of only one thing: unemployment. The rest he could deal with. Morrison remembers him as a proud, loving man devoted to his family, but also as a pessimist in terms of the broader culture. He has grown up in the South, in Klan-infested Georgia, and he nurtured a lifelong distrust of whites. Morrison claims that she "grew up in a basically racist household with more than a child's share of contempt for white people." But her father's distrust and his righteous anger were more protective than corrosive in her account, and they gave her a familial defense against the power and hegemony of the dominant white culture. In him she saw a person defining his life on his own terms rather than on somebody else's, regardless of his limited economic or political capital. His example and his love for her nourished her throughout her life. Nourishment, she believed, comes not just from women, but also from men.

Her mother held out greater hopes for whites. She had herself been raised by a father who doubted the possibility of change and a mother who believed in it. Morrison claimed that her own authority and voice were not self-invented but drawn from her female ancestors, passed down between women, generation to generation. She was, she said, fortunate in having descended from a line of strong, wise, resourceful women. Her great-grandmother was a midwife, to whom people came from far and wide to seek assistance in childbirth. Her grandfather, an "unreconstructed black pessimist," had

had his mother's land stolen from him and had been forced to support his family by traveling around, playing the violin. Although he was a very skilled carpenter and farmer, no one would hire him because of his race. His wife listened to his sad music but eschewed his despair, his insistence on the "repetition of the grotesque" in their people's history.

Morrison's grandmother believed instead in the slow but "miraculous walk of trees" from the valley up into the mountains, in the prospect of slow but "irrevocable and permanent change." This belief gave her the courage to flee the South, where her family had been reduced to sharecropping, and to head north with her seven children to be reunited with her husband and to start a better life for her family. Morrison, observing all these different familial attitudes, grew up with a sense of "racial vertigo," with a hope dirtied by despair and an anger sullied by optimism.

She never saw her birth as a new beginning that effectively cut her off as a separate piece from a whole cloth. The people whose bodies she had been born out of lived with her and in her; they would find their way into her work in various ways. As she grew up, they provided unrivaled examples of how to love and how to survive in a hostile environment. Her family sang and told ghost stories. When they only had one book (the Bible), they read it five times, cover to cover. They built relationships with other people in the black community in Lorain while living in a tense coexistence with poor, working-class whites whom they knew were aiming to rise above them.

Morrison's parents taught her love, rebellion, resilience, and humor. They laughed when a landlord set fire to an apartment they were living in, because the rent was overdue, and they moved together into a new apartment like a burned-down home was no big thing. She describes her mother as "the type who tore eviction notices off the door." Her father was similarly resistant to the outside world. When Morrison had an issue with an employer in one of her first jobs, her father told her to do her work and then go home. Her life was with her family. Family was what mattered, and throughout her life it served as her moral, intellectual, artistic, and social foundation.

Growing up, she was taught to see herself as part of a black collective, but she'd also be pulled individually onto her own path, educationally, artistically, and professionally. Along the way, she developed an admiration for misfits and outlaws. In both art and motherhood, Morrison tried to reconcile competing archetypes and to find a freedom that would otherwise be denied to her. She could be both a culture-bearer for her people and her family, playing the role of responsible adult and fulfilling her duties, and she could also be an artistic innovator, imagining new novelistic possibilities and new, independent ways to live. She could be both the "nest and the adventure," both "inn and trail." There was no conflict; freedom and responsibility were reconcilable.

o o o

One of the ways Morrison both affirmed her inherited traditions and rebelled as a child was by converting to Catholicism at the age of twelve. She'd been raised in the local African Methodist Episcopal (AME) church, where her mother was a member. The AME church had been founded by blacks for blacks, and its members had included many prominent African American figures, including Sojourner Truth. But she was pulled away from the AME community toward Catholicism, a church with a very small black membership at that time, and an institution with a history of anti-black racism. She never publicly explained why she converted. Like much else in her life, these details were kept private. As her full biography remains to be written, one can only guess at what might have drawn her to the Catholic church. She spoke mostly of how her cousins were Catholic, and how as a girl she was "perfectly content with [Catholicism's] aesthetics."

In her insightful book on Morrison's spiritual life, Nadra Nittle surmises that Morrison was drawn to the feminine divine enshrined at the heart of Catholicism. Catholics venerated the Virgin Mary, a mother who gave birth, saw her son suffer, could not protect him, and was destined to watch as he was nailed to the cross. In Protestantism, Morrison had often observed, there was just the cross, two empty pieces of wood hanging perpendicular over the altar. Catholicism stayed close to the bleeding body, the gruesome crucifixion. A son's tortured body presides over Catholic worship, reminding believers that Jesus's bodily suffering opened up eternity for all of God's children. The Madonna—her grief, her body, her child—was likewise iconic, if typically placed to the side of the crucifixion. Catholicism's emphasis on mothers, bodies, miracles, and a lineage of saints that stretches far back into history like holy ancestors must have appealed to her. Later she'd say that black women "have held, have been given . . . the cross. They don't walk near it. They're often on it. And they've borne that, I think, extremely well."

Catholicism's magical sensibility also resonated with the syncretic, folkloric African American spiritual tradition that surrounded her as a kid. "Black people believe in magic," she'd later explain, the way the rest of the culture believes in germs. She was interested in "the strange stuff." Men fly in her novels, women are born without belly buttons, ghosts appear, and women age backward. Belief in magic had been greatly diminished in the modern world, she could see, and she was defiantly drawn to it from an early age as a form of discredited knowledge. Catholicism's miraculous mother and son, the extraordinary birth at its ritual heart, would inform and electrify her novels, providing her with a rich, imaginative storehouse.

At the age of twelve, Morrison converted. Conversion involved baptism, a rebirth through the church's holy waters. It also entailed a renaming. Other people give us names at birth, but in a chosen rebirth we can name ourselves, as Sojourner Truth and Friedrich Nietzsche did. Morrison chose a new name for herself: Anthony. She established thereby her kinship with Saint Anthony of Padua, a Portuguese saint born in 1195 who was known for his scriptural literacy, powerful sermons, connections to Africa, and commitment to helping the poor and oppressed. When Morrison was in college, that baptismal name would be shortened to Toni, and the nickname would stick. She would remain a Catholic for the rest of her life, but she would define it on her own terms, outside the bounds of any orthodoxies.

o o o

Morrison excelled as a student, and she loved to read, devouring literary classics by Mark Twain, Leo Tolstoy, and Fyodor Dostoyevsky, among many others. She admired novelists who, out of the political particulars of their own time and place, their own gender and race, had written stories of broad human concern. She was admitted to Howard University in 1949 and moved away from home and family to attend college, a place she both grew in and felt dissatisfied by. At the time, the Howard curriculum focused on a white canon. She was also frustrated by the university's colorism and its racial hierarchies, and was disturbed by DC's segregated buses. But she appears to have thrived academically and socially. She majored in English, minored in Classics, acted, was runner-up for homecoming queen, and became the dean of pledgees for Alpha Kappa Alpha sorority. American poet Amiri Baraka watched her at Howard from afar with a sense of awe, describing her as "one of the most beautiful women I'd ever seen." She was an arresting presence on campus; he was too shy to approach her.

But despite Morrison's strong presence, part of her was elsewhere. DC never gripped her. One of the most formative experiences she had during those years did not happen on campus. It was a trip she took through the South with her acting troupe, through the landscape her ancestors had inhabited. She was greatly moved by the strangers who took her in as she traveled. Many of them were members of various churches, and she remembered the familial comfort she felt among them, sleeping in their welcoming houses and eating their home-cooked meals.

Already she was hungry for something other than what DC could provide, something deeper and more far-reaching in terms of her own intellectual and moral growth, something that had more to do with her own people—black people, but also people outside cities and mainstream cultural centers, women and the discredited, religious people and the traumatized veterans of wars, the disabled, single moms, and pregnant teenage girls. Children too. She was always interested in "what moves at the margin," and those margins, those movements, would clarify her sense of what was wrong in America and what was needed to set it right. By 1985 she would define the work she knew needed to be done in America: "it is nothing less than to alter the world in each of its parts: the distribution of money, the management of resources, the way families are nurtured, the way work is accomplished and valued, the penetration of the network that connects these parts." Needless to say, this was a bit much for a college student to take on. But her sense that a deep, fundamental transformation of the whole culture was needed—and might even be possible—grew in her.

From Howard, she went to graduate school at Cornell University, where she wrote a master's dissertation on William Faulkner and Virginia Woolf's treatment of the alienated. Three years after graduating and beginning her career as a university teacher in 1955, she married a Jamaican architect named Harold Morrison. What is striking in the written record she left behind, and in the many interviews she gave over the years, is how little she spoke about this stretch of time, the time roughly between her conversion to Catholicism and her experiences giving birth in the 1960s. This was the period in which she was out in the world on her own. These may have been enormously rich years for her, but in terms of what she shared publicly, they are less emphasized than her childhood years.

In her own narration, the story of her adulthood really begins after the birth of her first son, Harold Ford, in 1961. She publicly shared no details of the birth itself, but the event appears to have set in motion a consequential sequence of events. Around this time, Morrison joined a writers' group. Then in her early thirties, she had no dreams of becoming a writer, but the group provided stimulation and company and it gave her a chance to work through a memory from her childhood that had long haunted her. She remembered how as a child she'd had a friend, a young black girl, who had claimed she had solid proof that God didn't exist. Morrison, a firm believer, pressed the girl: what proof could she possibly have? The proof, she explained, was that she had prayed devotedly to God for blue eyes, but blue eyes had never graced her face.

What hatreds, external and internal, Morrison wondered, had fed this awful wish, had fueled this little girl's alienation from her own body, had led her to see prayer as wish fulfillment and God as some mercurial aesthetician? Morrison's literary ambitions were kindled there, in that informal writing group, by her desire to wrestle with that memory and this question, the pressures of which may have been made more acute by the birth of her son. How might she save him from such self-loathing, such "psychological murder," she may have wondered. How could she nurture his self-regard? She couldn't save that childhood acquaintance, but her son was in her care.

As she worked on the story, about two or three years after her first son's birth, she became pregnant again, and she and her husband decided to take a trip to Europe with young Harold. She never shared the details of that trip publicly, but it is well known that she returned home a single woman. Her marriage was over, and she would never marry again. With the due date fast approaching, she traveled back to Lorain and gave birth to her second son, Slade Kevin, in 1965, surrounded by her family. Her family supported her and her sons through the postnatal period until she took a job working for a textbook publisher and moved to upstate New York.

Newly employed, she found herself alone with her young sons in a cold and remote Syracuse. That is where she began writing in earnest. At night, as the children slept, she wrote as a salve for her depression and to blunt the edges of her loneliness as a single working mother in a city where she didn't know anyone. As she wrote, she populated her world with the people she had grown up among in Lorain, bringing that vibrant community to life on the page. This imaginatively remained her village, even if she had left it.

Her experiences giving birth spurred her creatively forward, inspiring her to write. They returned her to the community she had been born into, to the setting of her own birth and to the theme of birth more generally. Birth would be integral to her artistic vision, both conceptually and narratively, from her first novel through to her last.

She'd confess in interviews that single motherhood was enormously challenging and that she wouldn't have minded having a man around. But she was perfectly capable of making it work, with help from her parents and friends. When she felt overwhelmed, she remembered her grandmother, who had fled the South alone and broke with seven children in tow. That put sufficient wind in her sails, and she did what she needed to do. What she did in those years, of course, was much more than what most people accomplish in their lifetimes. Motherhood challenged her, but it also liberated her. "The real liberation," she said in a 2012 interview, "was the kids." She explained that their needs were simple. "One, they needed me to be competent. Two, they wanted me to have a sense of humor. And three, they wanted me to be an adult. No one else asked that of me. Not in the workplace—where sometimes they'd want you to be feminine, or dominant, or cute." "The kids didn't care if I did my hair, didn't care what I looked like."

That not caring what one looked like, and the love that grows between mother and child, the freedom Morrison found in that relationship, would work its way into the story she'd begun in that writing group, although these themes would appear there in reverse. Her story, which would blossom in Syracuse into her first novel, *The Bluest Eye*, begins with a pregnancy. The childhood acquaintance who had prayed for blue eyes became Pecola Breedlove, an eleven-year-old girl who greets the reader in the book's opening pages. The reader learns immediately that Pecola is pregnant with her father's baby and that the fetus inside her, like the marigolds planted in the unyielding earth that year, will shrivel up and die. Her baby, gestating in the aftermath of incest, will never be born. Morrison gives us no sentimental or whitewashed version of birth, but birth at the furthest moral, psychological, and physical reaches of human life, challenging her readers to see the humanity in a young girl full of self-loathing, a father who rapes his daughter, and a child conceived in violence, destined never to be born.

Lorain's black earth is unyielding in *The Bluest Eye*, but Morrison's own earth would prove to be more fertile. The creative seeds she had planted in the mud of her own loneliness quickly and fruitfully blossomed. She described her writing process as the construction of a womb of her own making, a womb protected from outside influences, within which she was "wholly free." Her kids were in that womb with her. She worked with and around them, but never in those early years without them. She wrote at night after they had gone to bed, or at 4 a.m. She could even write with them all around her, in the middle of the day. At first, she had tried writing in a separate room, behind a closed door, but this had frustrated them and their frustration kept her from writing. So she set up her desk right there in the room where they were playing. Interruptions were an integral part of her writing process; her style and stories would brim with a fullness, a sense of the collective, the chorus. They'd shift perspectives and make room for different narrators. She'd eschew the isolate, crystalline stillness that was part of a puritanical American aesthetic, the lone consciousness in dialogue with itself. She once described writing around some vomit her son had left on the page. She simply needed to get that sentence down before she forgot it. The wiping up could wait, but the sentence could not.

She somehow got her sentences down while raising her boys, moving to New York City, and building a distinguished list of books as a senior editor at Random House. *The Bluest Eye* came out in 1970 and was followed in quick succession by *Sula*, *Song of Solomon*, and *Tar Baby*, books that turned her into a bestselling author and a recipient of many distinguished prizes, including the National Book Critics' Circle Award.

She was at the height of her powers when she began working on *Beloved*, a book that sharply challenges the idea of motherhood as liberation and a novel with one of the most memorable birth scenes in all literature. *Beloved* is considered by many Morrison's masterpiece. It won the Pulitzer Prize, among other awards, and soon after its publication she was offered a distinguished endowed position at Princeton University. Four years later, she was awarded the Nobel Prize in Literature, the first black woman to win it. By the time *Beloved* came out in 1987, her sons were grown men in their twenties, and her country's political landscape was being dramatically realigned by the issues of birth, gender, and race.

o o o

Morrison's previous books had grown out of her own memories. But *Beloved* is based on a historical character: Margaret Garner, a nineteenth-century fugitive slave who escaped from Kentucky with her four children. Morrison discovered her in an 1851 newspaper clipping and spent three years researching and thinking about her story before setting her own version down on paper. The historical Garner arrived in Cincinnati with slavecatchers on her trail and, fearing her children would be caught and returned to a life of brutal enslavement, she tried to kill them. "I will not let those children live how I have lived," she said. She succeeded in killing one and was arrested—and charged with property theft rather than murder. The abolitionists swept in and became involved in her case, seeing in it a chance to advance their cause. They contested not her arrest but her charge; she should have been arrested for murder, the abolitionists argued. The law did not regard her children as people, merely as property. She, too: merely property. The law robbed her of her motherhood, and thereby of the heinousness of her own crime.

Morrison saw in Garner an example of maternal love pushed to its farthest reaches. What would someone do in such a situation? How can one even think about this question, how can one fairly evaluate her actions? Morrison was struck by how Garner conducted herself serenely and with tranquility throughout the proceedings. She also noticed the ambivalence of Garner's mother-in-law's response, as if she was disinclined to judge: "I watched her and I neither encouraged her nor discouraged her." What was clear to Morrison was that Garner loved her children deeply. Too deeply, perhaps. They were "the best part of her and she would not see them sullied."

Morrison clearly sympathized with Garner, perceiving her great love. At the same time, she was troubled by any refusal to judge her. What she had done was, in Morrison's opinion, "terrible," "unconscionable," "harrowing," "monstrous," "inhuman," and "outrageous." To not judge her was to put her outside the bounds of human morality, to somehow absolve her of the expectations of motherhood. It was, in a way, to reinforce the law's position on who she was: someone unimaginable, outside the human community. Despite her horrific circumstances, Morrison wanted to see her as imaginable.

Beloved began to take shape when Morrison identified the one person whom she believed was entitled to judge what Garner had done and punish her appropriately: her dead daughter. In *Beloved*, Garner becomes Sethe, a slave woman on a Kentucky plantation called Sweet Home. Sethe has a mild owner who allows her to form a union with another slave, Halle, and, although they cannot marry, they have three children together. Sethe is pregnant every year and a fourth child is on its way when her owner dies and a cruel "schoolteacher" takes over the plantation. She and Halle try to escape and fail, but they manage to place their children on a fugitive slave train headed north. In retaliation, schoolteacher seizes her and beats her. He watches as his nephews or sons, whoever they were, rape her, nineteen years old and six months pregnant. The young men suckle her youngest child's milk from her breasts. She learns years later that Halle was tied up and forced to watch all this from a loft in the barn.

Determined, she flees again, making her way alone to the Ohio River, where she encounters Amy Denver, a white indentured servant who is trying to escape to Boston, all in search of velvet. Velvet, she explains, "is like the world was just born." Amy's mother died in childbirth and Amy had been expected to work for the family they were indentured to, to pay off her mother's life. The child Sethe is pregnant with, Denver, will eventually grow up and replay the scene that comes next, trying to inch as close as she can imaginatively to her own birth. Denver remembers "the details of her birth—that and the thin, whipping snow she was standing in, like the fruit of common flowers," all of which testify to the "magic of her birth, its miracle in fact."

The two outlaws, black and white, meet in the woods as night approaches. God only knows what will come next, they admit, and whether Sethe will survive the night.

She makes it. But she wakes convinced her baby is dead. Amy and Sethe steal a broken canoe with one oar, lots of holes, and two birds' nests. As they approach the river, Sethe goes into labor. The birth is almost instantaneous. Sethe gets onto all fours in the canoe, which rocks with the dark water under it. She pants under four summer stars, throws her legs over the canoe's sides, and the baby's head comes out. *Push*, Amy yells. *Pull*, Sethe yells back. And then the rip. The "rip was a breakup of walnut logs in the brace, or of lightning's jagged tear through a leather sky." Denver is born, soon to be named after this improvising midwife who wraps her tenderly in rags. No one is there to observe the scene, to see or praise the very significant thing these women have just done together, and how they've done it so well: they've birthed a new human being. There Denver is, fresh with the uncompromised promise of her newborn life.

All around them, spores float in the water, looking like insects, but they are, Morrison tells us, the "seeds in which the whole generation sleeps confident of a future." Momentarily, one can believe that each spore will have a future, will "become all of what is contained in the spore: will live out its days as planned." But this moment doesn't last long.

Denver lives and Sethe is reunited with her family in Ohio, where happily, and very briefly (for twenty-eight days, or one menstrual cycle), she experiences the freedom needed to love her children fully, a love that had been impossible when she knew her children were not hers. Her mother-in-law, Baby Suggs, is an unchurched preacher and a mother of nine children and she leads the community in a Clearing. In that Clearing she proclaims, "Let the children come!" The children come, and they dance and cry with the women and men without restraint or guilt or shame. Baby Suggs beseeches them to love themselves, and to love their own hearts most of all—more than "your life-holding womb and your life-giving private parts." The heart is the prize. Their love is worth more even than their capacity to give life.

But the slavecatchers soon track Sethe down and she hides in a shed, where she runs the teeth of a saw under the chin of her third child, killing her to save her from the horrors she herself has lived through. This killing is an act of agency and of love for a woman stripped of agency and denied the privileges of love, but it isn't an act of liberation. Sethe's life seems to stop there; she lives in a state of arrested development, cut off from her community after she returns from prison. And years later, a young woman who appears to be her murdered child, now grown up, returns to haunt her as a hungry, demanding ghost.

"A woman loved something other than herself so much," Morrison marveled when she was writing the book. "She had placed all of the value of her life in something outside herself." That was a dangerous thing for a woman like her to do. Mother and daughter, birther and birthed, murderer and murdered, end up locked in a self-destructive dance of codependency, as if they "had arrived at a doomsday truce designed by the devil."

o o o

Over the years, many readers have criticized Morrison for writing more about exceptional people in exceptionally difficult circumstances than about average people leading ordinary lives. *Beloved* is often read as an extreme example of maternal love, of motherhood out on a dangerous limb. But historically, the circumstances Morrison described were more common than many people realize.

One of the authors Toni Morrison published at Random House, Angela Davis, would explicitly make the connection between Margaret Garner and other women of her era. In a remarkable essay published in the early 1980s, she explained that "reluctant acts of infanticide" were "common occurrences during slavery." In addition to killing newborn children, slave women frequently aborted fetuses when they realized they were pregnant. Plantation owners noticed that their female slaves had abnormally high rates of miscarriage. Maybe they were working too hard, or maybe, a physician proposed, they possessed a "secret by which they destroy the fetus at an early stage of gestation." At the time, abortion would have been a grave, rebellious sin not because it was murder, but because it was property theft. As Morrison wrote in *Beloved*, a slave woman's fertile body was "property that reproduced itself without cost."

"Black women," Davis affirmed, "have been aborting themselves since the earliest days of slavery. Many slave women refused to bring children into a world of interminable forced labor, where chains and floggings and sexual abuse for women were the everyday conditions of life." These infanticides and abortions were not acts of liberation; they were acts of desperation. They weren't choices so much as proof that such women lacked choices. Many of these women, Davis imagined, may have wanted to become mothers. Their acts were inspired not by birth's taxing biological process, but by the terrible conditions they lived under. "Most of these women," she argued, "would have expressed their deepest resentment had someone hailed their abortions as a stepping stone toward freedom."

Davis's essay was published nearly a decade after the United States Supreme Court's 1973 ruling in *Roe v. Wade*, which legalized abortion. The ruling was celebrated by many feminists as a triumphant culmination of the women's movement's long fight for equality, an unambiguous sign of progress. But many women of color, Davis argued, had felt less triumphant about it, even as they steadfastly believed that reproductive rights needed to be protected. Rather than the legal right to an abortion representing their freedom, they saw it as a reminder of the dire conditions that drove many women to abortion, and the ruling did nothing to fundamentally change those conditions. Additionally, black and Latino women in the U.S. had long been subject to extortionist abortionists seeking profit, and to forced abortions and sterilizations based on their race and class. In Sojourner Truth and Margaret Garner's era, again, black women weren't seen as mothers, and in the latter part of the twentieth century, the biases persisted. The rhetoric some feminists used to fight for the rights of disadvantaged women resonated eerily with that used by eugenicists: surely poor minority women wouldn't want to subject a next generation to their misery? The people making such arguments couldn't always imagine that a poor black family like Morrison's, one that had struggled to pay the rent, would have experienced the birth of their children as a joy, not a trauma. This was true even if childbirth was (and remains) exponentially more deadly for these women.

Other black women would similarly push back against the critique of motherhood that many of the more privileged white feminists took as a step in the direction of women's emancipation. "During the early stages of contemporary women's liberation movement," feminist critic bell hooks wrote in her influential 1984 book *Feminist Theory*, "feminist analyses of motherhood reflected the race and class biases of participants." For white middle- and upper-class women, childbirth and motherhood were identified as the locus of their oppression. They resented being tied to the home and to the endless cooking, cleaning, and childcare that went on in that home. They wanted to throw off that yoke and get out into the world. But if black women had raised their voices, she argued, motherhood "would not have been named a serious obstacle to our freedom as women." Such women saw the work they did in their families as "humanizing labor, work that affirms their identity as women, as human beings showing love and care." bell hooks never had children herself, but she believed that how we treat and value children matters greatly. This didn't translate into a "pro-life" stance. She wrote about how one can be personally against abortion in one's own life, but still committed to protecting the reproductive rights of other women.

Around this time, in 1983, bisexual American novelist, poet, and activist Alice Walker published her landmark book *In Search of Our Mothers' Gardens*, a collection of the "womanist prose" she'd been writing since the 1960s, dedicated to her only daughter. In the book's opening, she defined "womanist" against "feminist." If feminism was a movement largely of white women advocating for women's rights and equality, womanists came by and large from the black community and were "committed to survival and whole-ness of entire people, male and female." "Womanist is to feminist as purple to lavender," Walker wrote. A womanist was a woman who was grown-up, responsible, in charge, capable. She was "outrageous, audacious, courageous or willful." She was a lover of life; her many loves included music, dance, the moon, the spirit, love itself, food, roundness, struggle, the "folk," and herself.

A few years earlier, in an interview with Adrienne Rich, Audre Lorde, who described herself as "black, lesbian, mother, warrior, poet," likewise celebrated motherhood for its fecundity and human-ity. Inside all people, she believed—black and white, male and female—there is a black mother, a fruitful source of power and pos-sibility. The human species would evolve through women, but "we must never close our eyes to the terror, to the chaos which is Black which is creative which is female which is dark which is rejected which is messy... Sinister, smelly, erotic, confused, upsetting."

Examples from this period abound; there may have never been a more fruitful flowering for natality in the English language. The confluence of the women's movement, the fight for racial justice, and the postwar years produced one of the richest periods in the history of writing about birth. Lucille Clifton, a mother of six and a poet enthusiastically championed by Toni Morrison, would write one of the deepest and most discerning poetic testaments to birth during this era, authoring poems to her uterus and her period, poems about mothers and abortions, the unborn and living children, humans and their creative gods, Eve and Mary. "come coil with me," she invites her reader, "here in creation's bed." "this creation is so fierce," she wrote in a poem about Adam, "i would rather have been born."

For all she wrote about birth, Morrison said little about abortion, which is surprising given how little she shied away from controversial subjects. *Beloved*, however, reads as an exploration of abortion's dense and conflicted grounds, a reading Morrison may or may not have approved of. Does a mother have a right to determine what happens to her children? Is killing a child morally defensible when that child seems destined for a life of suffering? What are the moral and psychological costs of the loss of any child's life?

You don't find Morrison in the ranks of abortion's most vocal or militant campaigners, but *Beloved* points to her likely position. Women forced into a corner have only terrible choices; infanticide was not an act of liberation but an indictment of the culture that presented it as the most viable choice. Morrison knew she would need to affirm the life of her children. The dominant culture would not do this for them. She could not have devalued their life in the womb, have seen it as something easily discarded, heir as she was to a history of systematic human devaluation. She also knew that civilization needed those next children if her people would continue the slow walk of trees up mountains, the miraculous progress that her grandmother had prophesied.

Morrison welcomed in the children that others thought didn't stand a chance. She shocked many by talking positively in a 1989 interview about teenage pregnancies. Teenagers, she argued, have bodies that are ready to have babies. "Nature wants it done then, when the body can handle it," not at thirty or forty, when one is established in terms of finances, a career, or a stable nuclear family. Birth meets us in our precarity, she believed, and a child arrives.

This could all work out fine if we understood ourselves in terms of units more expansive than the individual or the isolated, self-enclosed nuclear family. Speaking of those teenage mothers, she said she personally wanted to take them in her arms and tell them, "Your baby is beautiful and so are you."

Morrison had, again, described Garner's infanticide as "terrible," "unconscionable," "harrowing," "monstrous," "inhuman," and "outrageous," but she also saw it as a remarkable act of agency by a woman denied all forms of agency. She could judge Garner's act, but she could simultaneously understand its logic; Garner believed that she and her child would be reunited on the other side of life, and her maternal love was greater than the drive to simply preserve life. Hannah Arendt had likewise cautioned against any ideology that had as its supreme and uncompromising ethos the preservation of the "biological life process," even in a citizenry stripped of all freedoms. "Politics," she wrote, "is never for the sake of life."

Morrison saw Sethe's infanticide as an assertion of her motherhood, not as a denial of motherhood. As a slave she had been a mere breeder who could make no claim to her children. But as a mother she claimed her children as her own flesh and blood, and she took responsibility for them. That simple claim of motherhood was in and of itself "illegal, anarchic." It was an "expression of intolerable female independence. It was freedom." Once that claim was connected to infanticide, it became "politically explosive."

Morrison also believed that life entailed living alongside the unconscionable, harrowing, monstrous, and outrageous. Isn't that what her people had been doing for centuries? Black people, she believed, were used to getting on with life when one's conditions and the actions they caused led one into morally fraught territory. Black people had mastered this art, of surviving and sometimes even thriving in terrible circumstances. "They had lived with various forms of evil all their days," she wrote in her 1973 novel *Sula*, "and it wasn't that they believed God would take care of them." Evil happened on God's watch. God had an evil brother, who hadn't spared God's son and wouldn't spare them either. This evil, however, wasn't separate from God. Evil was simply God's fourth face, and it was not something to run out of town or lynch, but "something to be first recognized, then dealt with, survived, outwitted, triumphed over." "We believe that evil has a natural place in the universe," Morrison wrote. "We try to avoid it or defend ourselves against it, but we are not surprised at its existence or horrified or outraged. We may, in fact, live right next door to it."

Because of her horrific crime, Sethe was an outsider in her community, but that community let her live next door, on its margins where she was free to work out her own slow and difficult salvation. Her crime may have been unforgivable, but her community would not destroy her. In fact, what bothered them most was not the crime itself but how Sethe had not turned to them for help as she rebuilt her life. Forgiveness was a community affair, and it required humble outreach and gracious reception.

So much analysis of *Beloved* has focused on the murdered child and the vengeful ghost that she becomes, and it is easy to forget the second daughter in the novel: Denver. Denver has lived because her mother has lovingly raised her. As Sethe begins to deteriorate, she in turn is saved by a desperate Denver, who reaches out to the community and begins the process of rebuilding bridges with the outer world, collecting food donations and sharing her story with other women. The novel ends with Denver and thirty community women outside Sethe's house, praying for her and ready to participate in her redemption. Sethe's "beautiful, magical best thing" was her children, and one of those children, a daughter who was born in a river halfway to Sethe's freedom, is still alive. She opens the door to their shared future. Meanwhile Beloved, who disappears after this scene, is last seen pregnant, her "belly big and tight" with, perhaps, some "beautiful, magical best thing" of her own.

o o o

Close to a decade after *Beloved* was published, on the cusp of the twenty-first century, Toni Morrison delivered a lecture in which she confessed that she feared for humanity's future. The future, she believed, was contracting in the West's collective imagination. Time was closing itself to the species that created it, organized it, a species that was increasingly looking backward, deep into time, but rarely forward. The human eye had been trained "on the biological span of a single human being." People could speak of *their* children, but not of all children, born into a future no single person would live to see. Humans could think forward only a few generations at best; after that, the horizon had become impenetrable to the human imagination.

But time, she resolutely and defiantly believed, had a future. That future entailed generations, connected one after the other like Hebrew Bible lineages, with births acting as fertile renewals. History, she prophesied, "is about to take its first unfettered breath." The future would be hospitable to the human race, but it would demand of us that we think not just of our own children and of their children, following forward through our own family lines, but of all the children alive today and all the children that might be born.

Morrison believed that even a character like Sethe, who had lived under conditions of overwhelming duress, would have explicitly chosen to be born. She too would have eschewed the anti-natalism of Nietzsche's wise old Silenus, who had argued that "the best of

8

NATALITY

all things is . . . not to be born, not to *be*, to be *nothing*." Even Sethe would have agreed with Morrison that people are wrong when they say, "I didn't ask to be born." We *did* ask to be born, she believed. "That's why we're here. We have to do something nurturing that we respect before we go. We must. It is more interesting, more complicated, more intellectually demanding and more morally demanding to love somebody. To take care of somebody."

Morrison published six novels after *Beloved* and many books of criticism and essays. She became a full-blown literary celebrity. Oprah Winfrey turned *Beloved* into a movie, casting herself in the lead role of Sethe. She praised Morrison as "our conscience. Our seer. Our truth-teller." Barack Obama awarded her the Presidential Medal of Freedom. But late in her life, she spoke of both hope and regret, of the mistakes she had made and the lives she had lost. One of those lives was that of her son, Slade Morrison, who died of pancreatic cancer in 2010 when he was forty-five years old. He left behind a series of children's books he had co-authored with his mother. His death left Morrison speechless, she claimed, but somehow she kept writing and she continued to focus on birth and the lives of children. The world grieved on August 5, 2019, when, at the age of eighty-eight, Morrison passed away in a New York City hospital from complications of pneumonia.

Her last novel, *God Help the Child*, published five years after her son's death and four years before her own death, is framed by this quote from Luke's Gospel: "Suffer little children to come unto me, and forbid them not." Allow the children in, Jesus says in that gospel, and do not block their passage, however restricted it might be.

On that novel's first page, a baby is pulled out from between a woman's legs. The book deals with the trauma of the parental rejection that follows a birth, due to the skin color the child is born with—

a rejection that happens in the context of a racist culture. There are no celebratory balloons, no cheers of delight in the delivery room. "I hate to say it," the birthing mother confesses, "but from the very beginning in the maternity ward the baby, Lula Ann, embarrassed me." The baby's father, equally appalled by his newborn child, leaves his family and never returns. But the novel is not a story of unending trauma. It ends with the rejected child grown up and hopefully pregnant with her own child.

"Now she's pregnant," Morrison wrote on the book's last page. "Good move, Lula Ann. If you think mothering is all cooing, booties, and diapers you're in for a big shock." She continues, "Listen to me. You are about to find out what it takes, how the world is, how it works, and how it changes when you are a parent." "Good luck," she ends the book, "and God help the child."

The book is dedicated not to her deceased son, or to her living son, or to any specific child at all. Its dedication simply reads, "For You."

I like to imagine some child born thousands of years from now, growing up and one day getting pregnant herself. She'll open up *God Help the Child* to find the gift of those two simple words: "For You." Over millennia her family would have traveled through bodies and through history, through good and through many evils, through grace and through destitution, walking up mountainsides like trees, and birthing their way slowly, painfully, and joyfully forward in time. Morrison's testament to natality is meant for her child and it's also meant for her. It's meant for anyone ready to accept birth, to laugh with it and cry with it, and to discover through birth "what it takes, how the world is, how it works and how it changes."

"You," Morrison once wrote, "are the touchstone by which all that is human can be measured . . . You took the hands of the children and danced with them."

Epilogue

Hannah Arendt, Friedrich Nietzsche, Mary Wollstonecraft, Mary Shelley, Sojourner Truth, Adrienne Rich, and Toni Morrison were all shaped by birth and they in turn have shaped our collective understanding of what it means to be born human. With verve and imagination, they showed how each person, in simply being born, creates an opportunity for history to begin again. Birth helped them see how we are more than history's by-products; we are instead creative participants in history, nature, and time. A human is born a tiny, infinitesimal piece of some massive whole, but that macrocosm is not impervious to the smallness of our individual births. These thinkers shared their interpretations, stories, and arguments about birth with the world and their testaments to birth have been read by millions of readers across the globe over the last three centuries. Their broad and deep impacts provide proof of the big claims they made about the power of human agency.

Their visions of natality are particularly poignant today as fatalism, paralysis, doubt, cynicism, and despair have become prevailing features of twenty-first-century life. In their own eras, these thinkers were highly attuned to the power structures that bred such despondency, but in their struggles against those structures, they imagined responses other than defeat. Over the last decade, as a pessimistic mood has intensified globally and amid a series of historic crises, these thinkers' expressions of human natality have offered me a powerful alternative to nihilism. Their natalities promised no panaceas, no quick fixes for being human. They saw in birth some of the most intractable problems in human life, but they also glimpsed there a power and abundance and even the capacity for human freedom. That they collectively maintained a courageous, affirmative, and nondogmatic commitment to birth, not just *despite* these problems but often *because* of them, has buoyed me and sustained me through some of the deadliest years in modern history.

During this time, it was mortality, not natality, that dominated the news cycle. I finished this book during the second full winter of Covid-19. I was tying up loose ends against the background of mass death and a crumbling world order, with six and a half million dead from the pandemic in two years and the world on high alert, fearing a third world war after the Russian invasion of Ukraine. Humanity's death drive seemed unassailable. I listened to a litany of mass shootings in unimaginable places and to environmentalists' warnings about species extinctions. Suicide and murder rates spiked, and people ingested painkillers that took their lives. Americans stockpiled assault weapons as Europeans fretted over their aging populations. Whole families of refugees floated to watery graves on rickety rafts and people starved to death outside luxury storefronts. Bestseller lists expressed a bleak zeitgeist, as readers eagerly purchased books with titles like *It Ends with Us*, *Killing the Killers*, *How to Kill Your*

Family, *The Man Who Died Twice*, and *The Subtle Art of Not Giving a F*ck*. Global mortality rates rose, and fertility rates dropped to their lowest levels on record.

"Even in the darkest of times," Hannah Arendt wrote, "we have the right to expect some illumination." Through these years, in the quieter background of these calamities, I would still hear about them: babies being conceived, babies being born. I wondered who these babies would become, what they would make of their births, and what unprecedented piece of human history they would help create. Would they find a cure for cancer, for instance, or help save some endangered species? Or would they go on a senseless shooting spree, or detonate a nuclear bomb? I couldn't predict what they would do with their lives, big or small, creative or destructive, compassionate or vicious. But I knew these babies mattered; they were the members of my children's generation, and the world would soon be in their hands.

To experience birth, to witness it and even celebrate it while living amid death and destruction, was to experience a complex and dissonant truth. It was a truth so obvious as to be banal: that we are born, and we will die; or that we are natal creatures in a mortal world. And yet it was a truth not easily digestible, not packageable for quick consumption. It has been best expressed not in polemics but in poetry: "were we led all that way for / Birth or Death?" one of the Magi asks in T. S. Eliot's "Journey of the Magi." The Magi, returning from a difficult winter journey on which they witnessed the miraculous newborn Christ, return to their kingdoms no longer at ease in the "old dispensation" but without any vision for a dispensation that comes next. They never answer the question they ask of themselves in the poem, and perhaps that's because it is unanswerable: "were we led all that way for / Birth or Death?"

o o o

To illustrate this vexed relationship between our natality and our mortal contexts, Hannah Arendt used the metaphors of deserts and oases. The world, she argued in her posthumous collection *The Promise of Politics*, has always been a desert. It has always been full of empty and arid stretches where no life forms can grow. Modernity, in her account, was merely an intensification of those desert conditions. In modernity, we are forced to adjust ourselves to aridity and are made to feel there is something wrong with us when we struggle to adapt to inhuman conditions. Psychology, she argued, tries to adjust the self to these conditions, but in encouraging that accommodation it takes away the only hope we have: "that we, who are not of the desert though we live in it, are able to transform it into a human world." The great danger she saw, one abetted by psychology, is that we would become "true inhabitants of the desert," that we would start to feel at home there, rather than working to change those conditions and create environments more hospitable to human life.

These deserts, she believed, were socially, culturally, and politically dangerous places. In the desert's lifeless, arid stretches, the bonds between people wither. The erosion of those bonds leaves people isolated, and their collective fragmentation creates the ideal conditions for totalitarianism to spread. Totalitarianism, as she saw it, is a sandstorm that blows through the deserts of modernity. "These storms," she argued, "are totalitarian movements whose chief characteristic is that they are extremely well-adjusted to the conditions of the desert."

Amid this lifelessness and these sandstorms, however, one can find oases, wild profusions of life that sustain human life in inhuman conditions without reconciling people to those conditions. The oases are, Arendt argued, "those fields of life" which exist independent of politics. Love is an oasis and so is friendship. Oases are where new life is born and cultivated. Oases represent our intimacy and our privacy, the places where we live unheard and unseen by the masses. The public world, in contrast, is where we come together in our separateness as unique individuals to engage in the political project of building a shared human world. That world is inherently mortal; it is "always subject to the mortality of those who build it." But it is simultaneously natal, subject to "the natality of those who come to live in it." Hamlet was right, Arendt claimed, when he said, "The time is out of joint; O cursèd spite / That ever I was born to set it right!" The time is always out of joint, and each of us is born to set it right. We arrive with our natality into a mortal world, and that natality is what a human world depends on. The world needs beginners, people who are committed to its rebuilding. Our oases are where we prepare for that beginning, that birthing, that rebuilding.

Our oases feed us and sustain us, but they are not, Arendt believed, where the entirety of our lives can be lived. We can turn to them in our depletion for nurturance, but they are not ultimately sites for relaxation or easy escape. They aren't easy places at all, in fact. Oases are natal, life-giving sources, but they demand of us our courage, endurance, action, and passion. We suffer in those oases, just as we suffer in the birthing of any new thing. Sometimes we suffer even more there, in those fecund profusions, than in the totalitarian sandstorms that promise an escape from the difficulty of being human. Oases are not where one becomes a non-suffering being, but where one becomes "an active being." We learn how to act in these oases, how to harness our natality, and without them "we would not know how to breathe."

Arendt had borne close witness to her fellow countrymen's slaughter of their neighbors, friends, and even family members. She had walked through the twentieth century's annihilating sandstorms, and she had come out alive. She never lost a "shocked wonder at the miracle of Being" and even into her old age she continued to insist on her own natality, her ability to begin again. She stayed close imaginatively to her oases, to those places that taught her how to breathe and where she sensed the fields of life. What disturbed her was not only the culture of actual death she'd observed in the Holocaust; it was also the living death of those who "disappeared from the world" while still alive, as if in anticipation of the death that eventually would claim them. They disappeared into passive contemplation or the afterlife; they abandoned themselves in political movements that took them for half-dead, or they retreated into their own apathy, aversion, or fear. What they denied, when they withdrew like that, is how the fields of life are always still discoverable in every single human life. We just have to look for them.

We discover those fields, Arendt believed, through our passions, our pleasures, our suffering, and even our anger. We break through to them by "thinking without a banister," as she called it—by thinking without the guardrails of dogmas or ideologies, by approaching reality like it has just been born, and by asking the toughest and most seemingly unanswerable questions about human life: Why were we born? Why are we alive? Why is there something rather than nothing? Why are we somebodies rather than nobodies? "These questions," Arendt wrote, "may sound nihilistic," but they are instead "the antinihilistic questions asked in the objective situation of nihilism where no-thingness and no-bodyness threaten to destroy the world."

o o o

At a time of nihilism, when "no-thingness and no-bodyness" threatened to destroy the world, I spent time in the company of Hannah Arendt, Friedrich Nietzsche, Mary Wollstonecraft, Mary Shelley, Sojourner Truth, Adrienne Rich, and Toni Morrison. Their visions of natality were my difficult oases, profusions of life that were full of passion, courage, suffering, and endurance. In those oases, I saw Friedrich Nietzsche on his long solitary hikes in the mountains, believing that "the soil is still rich enough" for humanity to go on living. I observed Mary Wollstonecraft, mere months before her death in childbirth, with her "soul most alive to tenderness," sensing a reality pregnant with "resistless energy." I witnessed Mary Shelley, after the death of her newborn baby, waking to the horror of what she called "the filthy workshop of creation" and to how we are bound to "prosperity or ruin" only by "slight ligaments." I wondered at Adrienne Rich's passionate "will to change" and her "succession of brief, amazing movements." I watched Sojourner Truth "be the instrument" of some of the most momentous and consequential movements in the modern world. And I loved Toni Morrison for her "ancient properties," for how she did exactly what those women she had so lavishly praised had done before her: she "took the hands of the children and danced with them."

Life is under threat in the twenty-first century. Even as life expectancies have risen dramatically over the last few centuries, we still live close to death. But birth is constantly here with us too. Birth can never undo death or forestall its advance, but wrestling with our natality can keep us connected to our source: the miraculous fields of life. Birth can help us see our lives as a "mark of resistance," as Adrienne Rich called it, to the floods that will soon arrive. They will come eventually, she warned us, and they will take with them everything we love and everything we cannot ever save. But still, stone by stone, we build them: our cairns in these wastelands, marking the fields of life we found and tried to sustain. Rich marveled at "these painfully assembled / stones, in the shape of nothing / that has ever existed before."

Acknowledgments

I am grateful to my agent, Tina Bennett, for encouraging me on this journey so many years ago, and for her steadfast vision, creativity, intelligence, and enthusiasm throughout. Thank you as well to Eve Attermann and Rivka Bergman at William Morris Endeavor.

Thank you to the friends and colleagues who read drafts and provided invaluable feedback: Abbie Storch, Joyce Seltzer, Samantha Rose Hill, Mahri Leonard-Fleckman, Anne Snyder, and Norman Wirzba. Thanks as well to all the writers featured in this book, alive and dead, and to the publishers, archivists, editors, and others who supported their explorations of natality. A particular thanks to the authors whose books most informed my biographical sections: Elisabeth Young-Bruehl, Samantha Rose Hill, Julian Young, Sue Prideaux, Lyndall Gordon, Charlotte Gordon, Nell Irvin Painter, Hilary Holladay, Stephanie Li, Nadra Nittle, Carolyn C. Denard, and Danille Taylor-Guthrie.

A deep thanks to my brilliant editor, Jill Bialosky, for her long commitment to this subject, for supporting the project from its early days, and for responding so perceptively to drafts. Thank you to Drew Weitman for her expert help at each stage, and to Allegra Huston for the excellent, sensitive copyedit. I am grateful to everyone else at W. W. Norton who worked behind the scenes, and whose contributions remain invisible, even to me.

Thanks most of all to my husband, who was my first reader, babysitter, conversation partner, and constant support, and to my mother, father, and three children, who have taught me more about natality than anyone else.

Notes

INTRODUCTION

1 **"When she speaks, heaven shakes"**: *Enheduana: The Collected Poems of the World's First Author*, trans. Sophus Helle (New Haven: Yale University Press, 2023), 63.

2 **"Who can here declare it"**: *Hymns of the Rig Veda*, trans. Ralph T. H. Griffith (Benares: E. J. Lazarus, 1896).

3 **"from the time"**: Seneca, *How to Die: An Ancient Guide to the End of Life*, trans. James S. Room (Princeton: Princeton University Press, 2018), 106.

4 **"Remember to keep death daily"**: https://www.ewtn.com/catholicism/library/rule-9162.

4 **"amidst a mud of feces"**: Vanessa R. Sasson and Jane Marie Law, eds., *Imagining the Fetus: The Unborn in Myth, Religion, and Culture* (Oxford: Oxford University Press, 2009), 64.

4 **"I do not extol"**: Sasson and Law, *Imagining the Fetus*, 82.

4 **"The aim of art"**: Andrey Tarkovsky, *Sculpting in Time: The Great Russian Filmmaker Discusses His Art*, trans. Kitty Hunter-Blair (Austin: University of Texas Press, 1989), 43.

4 **"having a moment"**: Erika Hayasaki, "Death Is Having a Moment," *Atlantic*, October 25, 2013, https://www.theatlantic.com/health/archive/2013/10/death-is-having-a-moment/280777/.

8 **"the supreme capacity of man"**: Hannah Arendt, *The Human Condition*, 2nd ed. (Chicago: University of Chicago Press, 1958), 247.

8 **"1. birthrate"**: https://www.dictionary.com/browse/natality.

10 **"cynical 'realism'"**: Hannah Arendt, *The Origins of Totalitarianism* (New York: Harcourt, 1951), viii.

10 **"do not care"**: Arendt, *The Origins of Totalitarianism*, 459.

10 **"when the most elementary form"**: Arendt, *The Origins of Totalitarianism*, 475.

10 **"Ideologies"**: Hannah Arendt, "Ideology and Terror: A Novel Form of Government," *Review of Politics* 15, no. 3 (July 1953): 312.

10 **"unredeemably stupid fatality"**: Arendt, *The Origins of Totalitarianism*, 267.

10 **"whole of nearly three thousand"**: Arendt, *The Origins of Totalitarianism*, 434.

12 **"the lady who imposes silence"**: *Enheduana*, 63.

12 **"Why is an absurdity felt"**: Muriel Rukeyser, "A Simple Theme," *Poetry* 74, no. 4 (July 1949): 238.

12 **"There is a terrible fear"**: Rukeyser, "A Simple Theme," 239.

12 **"Speech is a selfish act"**: Anne Enright, *Making Babies: Stumbling into Motherhood* (New York: W. W. Norton, 2004), 11–12.

13 **"at the far end"**: Rachel Cusk, *A Life's Work* (New York: Picador, 2001), 111.

13 **"Woman has ovaries"**: Simone de Beauvoir, *The Second Sex*, trans. Constance Borde and Sheila Malovany-Chevallier (New York: Vintage, 2009), 5.

14 **"psychosexual distortions"**: Shulamith Firestone, *The Dialectic of Sex: The Case for Feminist Revolution* (New York: Farrar, Straus and Giroux, 1970), 9–10.

14 **"shitting a pumpkin"**: Firestone, *The Dialectic of Sex*, 181.

15 **"Hundreds of millions"**: Paul Ehrlich, *The Population Bomb* (New York: Ballantine, 1968), Preface.

15   **Self-described "Birthstrikers":** Elle Hunt, "Birthstrikers: Meet the Women Who Refuse to Have Children Until Climate Change Ends," *Guardian*, March 12, 2019.

15   **About 44 percent of Americans:** See Anna Brown, "Growing Share of Childless Adults in U.S. Don't Expect to Ever Have Children," Pew Research Center, November 19, 2021; Amanda Barroso, "With a Potential 'Baby Bust' on the Horizon, Key Facts About Fertility in the U.S. Before the Pandemic," Pew Research Center, May 7, 2021.

15   **In the UK:** https://www.ons.gov.uk/peoplepopulationandcommunity/birthsdeathsandmarriages/livebirths.

16   **Global fertility rates:** Christine Tamir, "G7 Nations Stand Out for Their Low Birth Rates, Aging Populations," Pew Research Center, August 23, 2019.

18   **"the most liberating thing":** Danille Taylor-Guthrie, ed., *Conversations with Toni Morrison* (Jackson: University Press of Mississippi, 1994), 270.

18   **"as original a masterpiece":** Louise Erdrich, *The Blue Jay's Dance: A Memoir of Early Motherhood* (New York: Harper Perennial, 2010), 146.

19   **"Be patient toward all":** Rainer Maria Rilke, *Letters to a Young Poet*, trans. M. D. Herter Norton (New York: W. W. Norton, 1934), 35.

19   **"What keeps you from":** Rilke, *Letters to a Young Poet*, 49.

19   **"try to love the questions":** Rilke, *Letters to a Young Poet*, 35.

20   **Controlling human populations:** Matthew Connelly, *Fatal Misconceptions: The Struggle to Control World Population* (Cambridge, MA: Belknap Press of Harvard University Press, 2008), 47.

23   **"had no tradition behind them":** Virginia Woolf, *A Room of One's Own* (New York: Harcourt, 1929), 76.

25   **"pry loose the rich":** Hannah Arendt, "Introduction," in Walter Benjamin, *Illuminations*, trans. Harry Zohn (New York: Schocken, 1968), 50–51.

CHAPTER 1: THE MIRACLE THAT SAVES THE WORLD

27   **"born on a Sunday evening":** Martha Cohn, *Unser Kind* diary, Arendt Papers, Library of Congress. Cited in Elisabeth Young-Bruehl, *Hannah*

Arendt: For Love of the World (New Haven: Yale University Press, 1982), xlvi. Translation is Elisabeth Young-Bruehl's.

28 **"mere existence":** Hannah Arendt, *The Origins of Totalitarianism* (New York: Harcourt, 1951), 300–301.

28 **"abstract nakedness":** Arendt, *The Origins of Totalitarianism*, 300.

29 **"We saw the first smile":** Young-Bruehl, *Hannah Arendt*, 13.

29 **The capital of East Prussia:** Christopher Clark, *Iron Kingdom: The Rise and Downfall of Prussia, 1600–1947* (Cambridge, MA: Belknap Press of Harvard University Press, 2006), 584.

29 **"good and patient:** Two quotes from Samantha Rose Hill, *Hannah Arendt* (London: Reaktion, 2021), 17–18. Author's translation of Martha Arendt, "Notre enfante," in Hannah Arendt, *A travers le mur: Un conte et trois parables*, ed. Karin Biro (Paris, 2017), 56.

30 **a happy, rich childhood:** Young-Bruehl, *Hannah Arendt*, 3.

30 **"sunny, cheerful child":** Hill, *Hannah Arendt*, 18.

30 **"acute capacity for observation":** From Martha Arendt's "Notre enfante," cited in Young-Bruehl, *Hannah Arendt*, 16.

30 **"absolutely protected":** *Vita Activa: The Spirit of Hannah Arendt*, directed by Ada Ushpiz (Zeitgeist Films, 2005).

31 **"It is almost impossible":** Four quotes from Arendt, *The Origins of Totalitarianism*, 267–69.

32 **"difficult":** Hill, *Hannah Arendt*, 23–25.

32 **"hidden king":** Hannah Arendt, "Martin Heidegger at Eighty," *New York Review of Books*, October 21, 1971.

32 **Some critics have seen:** Jenny Turner, "We Must Think!" *London Review of Books*, November 4, 2021.

33 **"the camps and vast palaces":** Hannah Arendt, *Love and Saint Augustine*, ed. Joanna Vecchiarelli Scott and Judith Chelius Stark (Chicago: University of Chicago Press, 1996), 49. (Translation is Arendt's.)

33 **"Let's go, my friends!":** All Marinetti quotes from Lawrence Rainey,

Christine Poggi, and Laura Wittman, eds., *Futurism: An Anthology* (New Haven: Yale University Press, 2009), 49–51.

34   **"burning and overwhelming violence"**: Rainey et al., *Futurism*, 52.

34   **"triumph of memory"**: Arendt, *Love and Saint Augustine*, 48.

34   **"Once called into existence"**: Arendt, *Love and Saint Augustine*, 53.

34   **"lost all concrete relevance"**: Hannah Arendt, *Between Past and Future* (New York: Viking, 1961), 6.

35   **"It was as if"**: Hannah Arendt, "Was bleibt? Es bleibt die Muttersprache," interview with Günter Gaus, 1964. In Gaus, *Zur Person* (Munich: Feder, 1964). The translation is provided in the subtitles in the online interview on YouTube posted by Philosophy Overdose, who notes, "The translation is my own, but parts also come from the published version by Joan Stambaugh." https://www.youtube.com/watch?v=dVSRJC4KAiE.

36   **"profound, cheeky, cheerful"**: Hill, *Hannah Arendt*, 55. Author's translation of Günther Anders, *Die Kirschenschlacht: Dialoge mit Hannah* (Munich: C. H. Beck, 2012).

36   **"Never again!"**: Hannah Arendt, interview with Günter Gaus, cited in Young-Bruehl, *Hannah Arendt*, 108.

37   **"Do you realize"**: *Within Four Walls: The Correspondence Between Hannah Arendt and Heinrich Blücher, 1936–1968*, ed. Lotte Kohler, trans. Peter Constantine (New York: Harcourt, 1996), 31.

37   **"when we were young"**: Both quotes from Hill, *Hannah Arendt*, 188.

38   **"a violent courage"**: Hannah Arendt, "We Refugees," *The Jewish Writings* (New York: Schocken, 2007), 267–68. Also see "Internment" chapter in Hill, *Hannah Arendt*, 82–90.

38   **"the soul overleaps"**: Hannah Arendt, *Men in Dark Times* (Boston: Mariner, 1968), 6. For more on Hannah Arendt and hope, see Samantha Rose Hill, "When Hope Is a Hindrance," *Aeon*, October 4, 2021.

38   **"a dangerous barrier"**: Samantha Rose Hill, "When Hope Is a Hindrance," *Aeon*, October 4, 2021.

39   **Some readers have been:** See Turner, "We Must Think!": "It's something

a bit like this 'treasure' that Arendt calls 'natality,' the fact of human birth and the possibility of new beginnings, and I have to say that I don't buy it and always feel a bit embarrassed when Arendt tries to palm it off."

40   "grimness of the present": Three quotes from Arendt, *The Origins of Totalitarianism*, vii–ix.

40   "Never has our future": Arendt, *The Origins of Totalitarianism*, vii.

41   "irritating incompatibility": Arendt, *The Origins of Totalitarianism*, viii.

42   "This beginning is": Arendt, *The Origins of Totalitarianism*, 478–79.

43   "are not born": Hannah Arendt, *The Human Condition* (Chicago: University of Chicago Press, 1958), 246.

43   "rebellion": Two quotes from Arendt, *The Human Condition*, 2–3.

44   "The primacy of contemplation": Arendt, *The Human Condition*, 15.

44   "The more man learned": Arendt, *The Human Condition*, 281.

44   "is not, cannot possibly be": Arendt, *The Human Condition*, 270.

44   "innerworldly asceticism": Arendt, *The Human Condition*, 251.

45   "Natality": Arendt, *The Human Condition*, 9.

45   "always appears": Three quotes from Arendt, *The Human Condition*, 178.

46   "the sheer bliss": Arendt, *The Human Condition*, 106.

47   "There is no lasting happiness": Arendt, *The Human Condition*, 108.

47   "tragic pleasure": Two quotes from Arendt, *Men in Dark Times*, 6.

47   "conscious pariah": Hannah Arendt, "We Refugees," *The Jewish Writings*, 274.

47   "dual Monarchy": Young-Bruehl, *Hannah Arendt*, xl.

48   "genius for friendship": Young-Bruehl, *Hannah Arendt*, xxxviii.

48   She enjoyed: https://samantharosehill.substack.com/p/order-champagne.

48   "we love the world": Two quotes from Arendt, *Between Past and Future*, 193.

48   "its most glorious": Arendt, *The Human Condition*, 247.

49   "festival of life": Hannah Arendt, *The Life of the Mind: The Ground-breaking Investigation on How We Think* (New York: Harvest, 1971), 1:94.

CHAPTER 2: THE SOIL IS STILL RICH ENOUGH

51   "power and life": Hannah Arendt, *Between Past and Future* (New York: Viking, 1961), 34.

52   "God is dead": Friedrich Nietzsche, *The Gay Science: With a Prelude in Rhymes and an Appendix of Songs*, trans. Walter Kauffmann (New York: Vintage, 1974), 181.

52   "soil is still rich": Friedrich Nietzsche, *Thus Spoke Zarathustra*, in *The Portable Nietzsche*, ed. and trans. Walter Kauffmann (New York: Viking, 1954), 129.

53   "That there may be": Friedrich Nietzsche, *Twilight of the Idols*, in *The Portable Nietzsche*, 562.

53   "male mothers": Nietzsche, *The Gay Science*, 129.

53   "motherly human type": Nietzsche, *The Gay Science*, 337.

53   "premature births": Nietzsche, *The Gay Science*, 279.

54   "That which I am experiencing": Elisabeth Förster-Nietzsche, *Der junge Nietzsche* (Leipzig: Alfred Kröner Verlag, 1912), 14. Cited in Helmut Walther, "The Young Nietzsche," revised and expanded version of a lecture, Gesellschaft für kritische Philosophie Nürnberg, May 8, 2002, trans. Ingrid Sabharwal-Schwaegermann, http://www.f-nietzsche.de/djn_e.htm#FN6R.

54   "uncompromising materfamilias": Sue Prideaux, *I Am Dynamite!: A Life of Friedrich Nietzsche* (London: Faber and Faber, 2018), 9.

56   "delicate, kind": Friedrich Nietzsche, *Ecce Homo*, trans. Walter Kauffmann (New York: Vintage, 1967), 222.

56   "committed to the womb": Three quotes from *Nietzsche Werke: Kritische Gesamtausgabe*, ed. G. Colli and M. Montinari (Berlin: de Gruyter,

1967–2006), 1.1 4[77]. Cited in Julian Young, *Friedrich Nietzsche: A Philosophical Biography* (Cambridge: Cambridge University Press, 2010), 9–10.

56   **"hammer blows from heaven":** *Nietzsche Werke,* 1.1 4[77]. Cited in Young, *Friedrich Nietzsche,* 10.

56   **"liberty and lightness":** Prideaux, *I Am Dynamite!,* 10.

56   **"precocious, shy, affectionate":** Young, *Friedrich Nietzsche,* 20.

57   **"I am . . . already dead":** Nietzsche, *Ecce Homo,* 222.

57   **"father-house":** Young, *Friedrich Nietzsche,* 9.

57   **"the most blessed festival":** *Nietzsche Werke,* 1.1 4[77]. Cited in Young, *Friedrich Nietzsche,* 19.

58   **"beer materialism":** *Nietzsche Briefwechsel: Kritische Gesamtausgabe,* ed. G. Colli and M. Montinari (Berlin: de Gruyter, 1975–2004), 1.2 467. Cited in Young, *Friedrich Nietzsche,* 53.

58   **"earth is a place":** *Nietzsche Werke,* 1.4 35 [I]. Cited in Young, *Friedrich Nietzsche,* 57.

60   **On Nietzsche's second visit:** See Oliver Hilmes, *Cosima Wagner: The Lady of Bayreuth,* trans. Stewart Spencer (New Haven: Yale University Press, 2010), 112. Also see Prideaux, *I Am Dynamite!,* 61–62.

60   **"good omen":** Two quotes from Prideaux, *I Am Dynamite!,* 62.

61   **"confusion of genius-creating":** *Nietzsche Briefwechsel,* 11.2, To Nietzsche, 16. Cited in Young, *Friedrich Nietzsche,* 107.

61   **"a governess, a nurse":** Young, *Friedrich Nietzsche,* 106.

61   **"still-born creature":** *Nietzsche Briefwechsel,* 11.3 309. Cited in Young, *Friedrich Nietzsche,* 168.

61   **"days of trust":** Nietzsche, *Ecce Homo,* 247.

62   **"bloody soil":** Nietzsche to Carl von Gersdorff, December 12, 1870. Cited in Prideaux, *I Am Dynamite!,* 80.

62   **"all man can now see":** Friedrich Nietzsche, *The Birth of Tragedy: Out*

of the Spirit of Music, trans. Shaun Whiteside and ed. Michael Tanner (New York: Penguin, 1993), 40.

62 **"Miserable, ephemeral race":** Nietzsche, *The Birth of Tragedy,* 22.

62 **"in this supreme menace":** Nietzsche, *The Birth of Tragedy,* 40.

63 **"mysterious primal Oneness":** Nietzsche, *The Birth of Tragedy,* 17.

63 **"unbounded lust":** Nietzsche, *The Birth of Tragedy,* 80.

63 **"'the shining one'":** Nietzsche, *The Birth of Tragedy,* 16.

63 **"wretched belljar":** Nietzsche, *The Birth of Tragedy,* 101.

64 **"the embodiment of disgust":** Nietzsche, *The Birth of Tragedy,* 9.

65 **"During each fleeting recuperation":** Prideaux, *I Am Dynamite!,* 202.

65 **Julian Young guesses:** Young, *Friedrich Nietzsche,* 559–62.

65 **"*dual* series of experience":** Nietzsche, *Ecce Homo,* 225.

65 **"human, all too human":** *Human, All Too Human* was the title of a book Nietzsche published in this period, in 1878.

66 **"From what stars":** Two quotes from Prideaux, *I Am Dynamite!,* 199.

66 **"deep inner life":** Two quotes from *Friedrich Nietzsche: Chronik in Bildern und Texten,* ed. R. Benders and S. Oettermann (Munich and Vienna: Hanser, 2000), 510. Cited in Young, *Friedrich Nietzsche,* 341.

66 **"Monte Sacro—":** *Nietzsche Briefwechsel,* III 7/1, 905. Cited in Young, *Friedrich Nietzsche,* 342.

67 **"Would you not throw":** Nietzsche, *The Gay Science,* 273–74.

67 **"immoral":** Two quotes cited in Prideaux, *I Am Dynamite!,* 235.

67 **"disgrace to his father's grave":** Cited in Young, *Friedrich Nietzsche,* 353.

67 **"Alas, this pregnant nocturnal dismay":** Nietzsche, *Thus Spoke Zarathustra,* in *The Portable Nietzsche,* 266.

69 **"blood-letting":** *Nietzsche Briefwechsel,* III.I 403, as cited in Young, *Friedrich Nietzsche,* 366.

69 **"dangerous across"**: Nietzsche, *Thus Spoke Zarathustra*, in *The Portable Nietzsche*, 126.

69 **"belly of being"**: Nietzsche, *Thus Spoke Zarathustra*, in *The Portable Nietzsche*, 144.

70 **"Man and woman"**: Nietzsche, *Thus Spoke Zarathustra*, in *The Portable Nietzsche*, 322.

70 **"Everything... about woman"**: Two quotes from Nietzsche, *Thus Spoke Zarathustra*, in *The Portable Nietzsche*, 178.

70 **"Never yet have I found"**: Nietzsche, *Thus Spoke Zarathustra*, in *The Portable Nietzsche*, 340–43.

70 **"birth to lightning bolts"**: Nietzsche, *Thus Spoke Zarathustra*, in *The Portable Nietzsche*, 401.

70 **"umbilical cord of time"**: Nietzsche, *Thus Spoke Zarathustra*, in *The Portable Nietzsche*, 334.

70 **"Whoever has to give birth"**: Nietzsche, *Thus Spoke Zarathustra*, in *The Portable Nietzsche*, 403.

71 **"three metamorphoses"**: Three quotes from Nietzsche, *Thus Spoke Zarathustra*, in *The Portable Nietzsche*, 137–39.

71 **"I say unto you"**: Two quotes from Nietzsche, *Thus Spoke Zarathustra*, in *The Portable Nietzsche*, 129.

71 **"Alas... the time is coming"**: Nietzsche, *Thus Spoke Zarathustra*, in *The Portable Nietzsche*, 129.

72 **"Speak to me"**: Nietzsche, *Thus Spoke Zarathustra*, in *The Portable Nietzsche*, 395.

72 **"My children ... are near"**: Nietzsche, *Thus Spoke Zarathustra*, in *The Portable Nietzsche*, 438.

73 **"the patient asks often"**: Cited in Prideaux, *I Am Dynamite!*, 332.

73 **"The triumphant Yes"**: Nietzsche, *Twilight of the Idols*, in *The Portable Nietzsche*, 561–62.

73   **"at bottom I am"**: Two quotes from Nietzsche, *Letters (1889)*, in *The Portable Nietzsche*, 686.

74   **"At the head"**: Elisabeth Förster-Nietzsche, unpublished letter, May 12, 1933. Cited in Prideaux, *I Am Dynamite!*, 370.

75   **"We owe some of our"**: Louise Erdrich, *The Blue Jay's Dance: A Birth Year* (New York: Harper Perennial, 1995), 148.

76   **"This wild avarice"**: Nietzsche, *The Gay Science*, 89.

76   **"as by a gruesome"**: Four quotes from Nietzsche, *The Gay Science*, 127–28. Thank you to Sue Prideaux for drawing my attention to this passage.

76   **"I fear I've made"**: Erdrich, *The Blue Jay's Dance*, 9.

77   **"the mystery of an epiphany"**: Erdrich, *The Blue Jay's Dance*, 148.

CHAPTER 3: THE SOUL MOST ALIVE TO TENDERNESS

79   **"resistless energy"**: Two quotes from Mary Wollstonecraft, "On Poetry, and Our Relish for the Beauties of Nature," Women Writers Online, https://wwo.wwp.northeastern.edu/WWO/search?browse-all=yes;brand=wwo#!/view/wollstonecraft.poetry.xml.

80   **"a blueprint for human change"**: Lyndall Gordon, *Vindication: A Life of Mary Wollstonecraft* (New York: Harper Perennial, 2005), 2.

80   **"the first of a new"**: *The Collected Letters of Mary Wollstonecraft*, ed. Ralph M. Wardle (Ithaca, NY: Cornell University Press, 1979), 164. Cited in Gordon, *Vindication*, 2.

81   **In eighteenth-century England:** See Charlotte Gordon, *Romantic Outlaws: The Extraordinary Lives of Mary Wollstonecraft and Mary Shelley* (New York: Random House, 2015), 62, 65, 429. Also see Gordon, *Vindication*, 10–11.

81   **"little platoon"**: See Eileen M. Hunt, "The Family as Cave, Platoon and Prison: The Three Stages of Wollstonecraft's Philosophy of the Family," *Review of Politics* 64, no. 1 (Winter 2002): 83.

82   **"an active agent"**: Virginia Woolf, "Mary Wollstonecraft," *The Common Reader*, second series (New York: Harcourt, Brace, 1935).

82   **"I will not marry"**: Cited in Gordon, *Vindication*, 30.

82   **"fits of phrensy"**: Mary Wollstonecraft to Everina, c. late 1783, *The Collected Letters of Mary Wollstonecraft*, 39. Cited in Gordon, *Vindication*, 31.

83   **extremely depressed**: See Gordon, *Vindication*, 62.

83   **"I am now beginning"**: Two quotes from *The Collected Letters of Mary Wollstonecraft*, 100–101. Cited in Gordon, *Vindication*, 65.

84   **"*study* the scenes of sorrow"**: John Hewlett, *Sermons* (London: Rivington & J. Johnson, 1786). Cited in Gordon, *Vindication*, 71.

84   **"Keep thy heart"**: Reverend Mr. Hewitt's instructions, cited in Gordon, *Vindication*, 71.

84   **"loudly demands JUSTICE"**: Mary Wollstonecraft, *A Vindication of the Rights of Woman*, ed. Eileen Hunt Botting (New Haven: Yale University Press, 2014), 24.

84   **"affection for the whole"**: Wollstonecraft, *A Vindication of the Rights of Woman*, 21.

85   **"visiting the harlot"**: Two quotes from Wollstonecraft, *A Vindication of the Rights of Woman*, 24.

86   **"a propensity to tyrannize"**: Wollstonecraft, *A Vindication of the Rights of Woman*, 33.

87   **"I build my belief"**: Wollstonecraft, *A Vindication of the Rights of Woman*, 40.

87   **"Could the helpless creature"**: Wollstonecraft, *A Vindication of the Rights of Woman*, 39.

88   **"Liberty with maternal wing"**: Mary Wollstonecraft, *An historical and moral view of the origin and progress of the French Revolution; and the effect it has produced in Europe* (1795). Evans Early American Imprint Collection: https://quod.lib.umich.edu/cgi/t/text/text-idx?c=evans;idno=N22635.0001.001.

88   **"vigorous little Girl"**: Three quotes from Mary Wollstonecraft to Ruth Barlow, May 20, 1794. Cited in Gordon, *Vindication*, 230.

89   **"thick fetid pus"**: Randi Hutter Epstein, *Get Me Out: A History of Child-*

birth from the Garden of Eden to the Sperm Bank (New York: W. W. Norton, 2010), 53.

89 **In the eighteenth century:** Irvine Loudon, *The Tragedy of Childbed Fever* (Oxford: Oxford University Press, 2000).

90 **half of French babies:** Gordon, *Vindication*, 231.

90 **"in effect, wealthy parents":** Valerie A. Fildes, *Breasts, Bottles, and Babies: A History of Infant Feeding* (Edinburgh: Edinburgh University Press, 1986), 193.

91 **"trembled on the brink":** Mary Wollstonecraft, *Letters Written in Sweden, Norway, and Denmark*, ed. Tone Brekke and Jon Mee (Oxford: Oxford University Press, 2009), 11–12.

92 **"Paradise . . . was before me":** Wollstonecraft, *Letters Written in Sweden, Norway, and Denmark*, 66.

92 **"beings training to be sold":** Wollstonecraft, *Letters Written in Sweden, Norway, and Denmark*, 120.

92 **"in a living tomb":** Two quotes from *Godwin on Wollstonecraft: Memoirs of the Author of "The Rights of Woman,"* ed. Richard Holmes (New York: Harper Perennial, 2005), 65.

92 **"unwilling to cut":** Mary Wollstonecraft, letter to a friend. Cited in *Godwin on Wollstonecraft*, 66.

93 **"fitted to meet":** Woolf, "Mary Wollstonecraft."

94 **He believed in mind:** https://plato.stanford.edu/entries/godwin/.

94 **"little man":** Woolf, "Mary Wollstonecraft."

94 **"newborn peace":** *Godwin on Wollstonecraft*, 74.

95 **"worshipper of domestic life":** Two quotes from *Godwin on Wollstonecraft*, 77.

95 **"coming to birth in her":** Two quotes from Woolf, "Mary Wollstonecraft."

96 **"I begin to love":** Two quotes from Mary Wollstonecraft to William Godwin, June 6, 1797, in Wardle, *The Collected Letters of Mary Wollstonecraft*, 416–17. Cited in Gordon, *Vindication*, 348–49.

98 **"The silken wings":** Two quotes from Wollstonecraft, "On Poetry."

99 **"at the hazard":** William Godwin to Mary Wollstonecraft, June 1797, in *Godwin and Mary: Letters of William Godwin and Mary Wollstonecraft*, ed. Ralph M. Wardle (Lawrence: University of Kansas Press, 1966), 89.

100 **"too decayed a state":** *Godwin on Wollstonecraft*, 87.

100 **Her motherlessness:** See Lyndall Gordon, *Outsiders: Five Women Writers Who Changed the World* (Baltimore: Johns Hopkins University Press, 2017), 3.

101 **"high-handed and hot-blooded":** Woolf, "Mary Wollstonecraft."

Chapter 4: The Workshop of Filthy Creation

103 **"We think back through":** Three quotes from Virginia Woolf, *A Room of One's Own* (New York: Harcourt, 1929), 76–78.

104 **"vastness and variety":** Woolf, *A Room of One's Own*, 88.

104 **"unquestionably the most poetic":** Sandra M. Gilbert and Susan Gubar, *The Madwoman in the Attic: The Woman Writer and the Nineteenth-Century Literary Imagination* (originally published 1979; New Haven: Yale University Press, 2020), 25.

105 **"The memory of my mother":** *Selected Letters of Mary Wollstonecraft Shelley*, ed. Betty T. Bennett (Baltimore: Johns Hopkins University Press, 1995), 2:34. Used as an epigraph in Charlotte Gordon, *Romantic Outlaws: The Extraordinary Lives of Mary Wollstonecraft and Mary Shelley* (New York: Random House, 2015).

106 **"hyena in petticoats":** Lyndall Gordon, *Vindication: A Life of Mary Wollstonecraft* (New York: Harper Perennial, 2005), 4.

106 **"concubine":** *The Anti-Jacobin Review and Magazine* 1 (July–December 1798).

106 **"The child was born":** *Godwin on Wollstonecraft: Memoirs of the Author of "The Rights of Woman,"* ed. Richard Holmes (New York: Harper Perennial, 2005), 81.

107 **"As a child":** Mary Shelley, *Frankenstein: Or, The Modern Prometheus* (New York: Signet, 2013), 1.

107   **"an increaser"**: Edward S. Said, *Beginning: Intention and Method* (New York: Basic Books, 1975), 83. Cited in Gilbert and Gubar, *The Madwoman in the Attic*, 4.

107   **"a father, a progenitor"**: Gilbert and Gubar, *The Madwoman in the Attic*, 4.

108   **"legislators"**: Percy Bysshe Shelley, *A Defence of Poetry and Other Essays*, available as an ebook from Project Gutenberg, https://www.gutenberg.org/files/5428/5428-h/5428-h.htm.

109   **"judge how far"**: Shelley, *Frankenstein*, 2.

109   **"communicate with unlimited freedom"**: Mary Shelley, diary entry, October 2, 1822, in *The Journals of Mary Shelley*, ed. Paula R. Feldman and Diana Scott-Kilvert (Baltimore: Johns Hopkins University Press, 1980), 429. Cited in Lyndall Gordon, *Outsiders: Five Women Writers Who Changed the World* (Baltimore: Johns Hopkins University Press, 2019), 9.

109   **"the mortal chain"**: Percy Bysshe Shelley, "*from* Laon and Cythna; or The Revolution of the Golden City," https://www.poetryfoundation.org/poems/56665/laon-and-cythna-or-the-revolution-of-the-golden-city.

111   **"I was a mother"**: Cited in Gordon, *Outsiders*, 33.

111   **"Dream that my little baby"**: Mary Shelley, diary entry, March 19, 1815, in *The Journals of Mary Shelley*, 70. Cited in Gordon, *Romantic Outlaws*, 133.

112   **"Life, the great miracle"**: Two quotes from Percy Bysshe Shelley, *A Defence of Poetry and Other Essays*.

112   **"Better to reign"**: John Milton, *Paradise Lost*, Book 1, lines 221–70.

113   **"workshop of filthy creation"**: Shelley, *Frankenstein*, 54.

113   **"mad, bad and dangerous"**: Cited in Gordon, *Romantic Outlaws*, 156.

113   **"the league of incest"**: Byron to John Cam Hobhouse, November 11, 1818, in *Lord Byron's Correspondence*, ed. John Murray (New York: Charles Scribner's Sons, 1922), 2:89. Cited in Gordon, *Romantic Outlaws*, 167.

113   **"principle of life"**: Shelley, *Frankenstein*, 5.

114   **"We will each write"**: Shelley, *Frankenstein*, 3.

114 **"felt that blank":** Shelley, *Frankenstein*, 4.

114 **"Invention . . . does not consist":** Shelley, *Frankenstein*, 4.

115 **"The significance of the novel's":** Three quotes from Gordon, *Romantic Outlaws*, 242–43.

116 **"perhaps a corpse":** Three quotes from Shelley, *Frankenstein*, 5.

117 **"I had selected":** Shelley, *Frankenstein*, 58.

118 **Perhaps the monster is Mary Shelley:** See Gilbert and Gubar, *The Madwoman in the Attic*, 213–47.

119 **"the bloom of health":** Three quotes from Shelley, *Frankenstein*, 59.

121 **"a part of the world":** Shelley, *Frankenstein*, 11.

122 **"Greece had not been":** Shelley, *Frankenstein*, 56.

122 **"I loved to imagine":** Two quotes from *The Letters of Mary Wollstonecraft Shelley*, ed. Betty T. Bennett (Baltimore: Johns Hopkins University Press, 1980), 1:291.

122 **"universal wreck":** Mary Shelley, *The Last Man* (Ware, UK: Wordsworth, 2004), 359.

122 **"I lived upon an earth":** Shelley, *The Last Man*, 310–13.

123 **"seedless ocean":** Shelley, *The Last Man*, 374.

123 **"The world was empty":** Shelley, *The Last Man*, 362.

123 **"They were all to me":** Three quotes from Shelley, *The Last Man*, 360–61.

123 **"the LAST MAN":** Shelley, *The Last Man*, 375.

124 **"rough beast":** William Butler Yeats, "The Second Coming," in *The Collected Poems of W. B. Yeats* (London: Wordsworth, 1994), 158.

124 **"Thus strangely are":** Shelley, *Frankenstein*, 41.

Chapter 5: To Be the Instrument

125 **"excavate a wound":** Saidiya Hartman, *Lose Your Mother: A Journey Along the Atlantic Slave Route* (New York: Farrar, Straus and Giroux, 2007), 40.

126 **"Every tale of creation"**: Hartman, *Lose Your Mother*, 110.

126 **"the dungeon was a womb"**: Hartman, *Lose Your Mother*, 111.

127 **"Gestational language"**: Hartman, "The Belly of the World: A Note on Black Women's Labors," *Souls: A Critical Journal of Black Politics, Culture, and Society* 18, no. 1 (January–March 2016): 166–73.

127 **"Adam and Eve"**: Two quotes from Hartman, *Lose Your Mother*, 110.

127 **"blood and shit"**: Hartman, *Lose Your Mother*, 110.

128 **Rosendale would eventually:** https://www.townofrosendale.com/rosendales-history/.

129 **"sit down under the sparkling"**: Two quotes from Sojourner Truth, *Narrative of Sojourner Truth*, ed. Nell Irvin Painter (New York: Penguin, 1998), 12.

130 **"put under the hammer"**: Truth, *Narrative of Sojourner Truth*, 12.

131 **"penniless, weak, lame"**: Truth, *Narrative of Sojourner Truth*, 14.

131 **"This faithful slave"**: Truth, *Narrative of Sojourner Truth*, 17.

133 **"Diana, born about"**: Nell Irvin Painter, *Sojourner Truth: A Life, A Symbol* (New York: W. W. Norton, 1996), 19.

133 **"in being permitted"**: Truth, *Narrative of Sojourner Truth*, 25.

134 **"dark imagery"**: Truth, *Narrative of Sojourner Truth*, 25.

134 **"moral gutter"**: The phrase "moral gutter" is used by Frances W. Titus in her preface to "Book of Life," the compilation she put together of accounts of Truth from various sources, interwoven with her own commentary. This is published alongside the *Narrative* in Truth, *Narrative of Sojourner Truth*, ed. Painter, 89.

135 **"I'll have my child"**: Truth, *Narrative of Sojourner Truth*, 30–31.

135 **"sees the end"**: Truth, *Narrative of Sojourner Truth*, 38.

135 **"God . . . is the great house"**: Truth, *Narrative of Sojourner Truth*, 7.

135 **"same spirit that was"**: Truth, *Narrative of Sojourner Truth*, 47.

137 **"testifying of the hope"**: Truth, *Narrative of Sojourner Truth*, 68.

137 **"Sojourner, robbed"**: Truth, *Narrative of Sojourner Truth*, 131.

137 **"with the tones"**: Truth, *Narrative of Sojourner Truth*, 75.

138 **"If the Lord comes"**: Truth, *Narrative of Sojourner Truth*, 76.

138 **"self-made woman"**: Truth, *Narrative of Sojourner Truth*, 3.

138 **"a tall imposing figure"**: George R. Stetson, "When I Was a Boy," 121, cited in Painter, *Sojourner Truth*, 95.

138 **"dignified"**: Truth, *Narrative of Sojourner Truth*, 3.

139 **"I Sell the Shadow"**: Painter, *Sojourner Truth*, 189.

140 **"set it right side"**: Painter, *Sojourner Truth*, 125.

140 **"God who created him"**: *Anti-Slavery Bugle* (Salem, MA), June 21, 1851, cited in Painter, *Sojourner Truth*, 126.

141 **"I have borne"**: Frances Dana Gage, "Ain't I a Woman," *Independent* (New York), April 23, 1863, cited in Painter, *Sojourner Truth*, 167.

141 **"told them that her breasts"**: *The Liberator* (Boston), October 15, 1858, cited in Painter, *Sojourner Truth*, 139.

142 **"Her skillful remaking"**: Both quotes from Painter, *Sojourner Truth*, 140.

142 **"They created an upbeat story"**: Toni Morrison, *The Source of Self-Regard: Selected Essays, Speeches, and Meditations* (New York: Alfred A. Knopf, 2019), 311.

144 **"vital spark"**: Truth, *Narrative of Sojourner Truth*, 89.

144 **"her religion is not tinctured"**: Truth, *Narrative of Sojourner Truth*, 83.

144 **"peered toward the future"**: Truth, *Narrative of Sojourner Truth*, 131.

145 **"We talk of a beginning"**: *Chicago Inter-Ocean*, January 1, 1881, cited in Painter, *Sojourner Truth*, 249.

145 **"This has become"**: *Christian Recorder* (Philadelphia), January 27, 1881, 4; *Woman's Journal* (Philadelphia), November 14, 1903. Both cited in Painter, *Sojourner Truth*, 249.

Chapter 6: The Will to Change

148 **"lofty and crippled":** Adrienne Rich, *On Lies, Secrets, and Silence: Selected Prose* (New York: W. W. Norton, 1976), 212.

149 **"I begin to imagine":** Adrienne Rich, *Of Woman Born: Motherhood as Experience and Institution* (New York: W. W. Norton, 1976), dedication.

149 **"jovial alcoholic":** Hilary Holladay, *The Power of Adrienne Rich: A Biography* (New York: Doubleday, 2020), 16.

149 **"opaquely smiling":** Holladay, *The Power of Adrienne Rich*, 15.

150 **"gardenia blanched":** Rich, *Of Woman Born*, 220.

150 **"born in my father's":** Adrienne Rich, "Split at the Root," *Blood, Bread, and Poetry: Selected Prose 1979–1985* (New York: W. W. Norton, reissue 1994), 101.

151 **"subliminal, subversive":** Rich, *Of Woman Born*, 220.

151 **"egotistical, tyrannical":** Rich, *Blood, Bread, and Poetry*, 113.

152 **"cataclysm":** Rich, *Of Woman Born*, 166.

152 **"If it is true":** Rich, *Blood, Bread, and Poetry*, 102.

153 **"nonexempt from":** Rich, *Blood, Bread, and Poetry*, 103.

153 **"every one of those piles":** Rich, *Blood, Bread, and Poetry*, 107.

154 **"messy, noisy, unpredictable":** Rich, *Blood, Bread, and Poetry*, 111.

154 **"recording the rebirth":** Rich, *Of Woman Born*, 25.

155 **"What new shapes":** Adrienne Rich, "A Change of World," in Rich, *Collected Poems: 1950–2012* (New York: W. W. Norton, 2016), 28.

155 **The world was indeed changing:** See Louis Menand, *The Free World: Art and Thought in the Cold War* (New York: Farrar, Straus and Giroux, 2021), 423.

158 **"Victorian Lady":** Rich, *Of Woman Born*, 27.

159 **"at the deepest levels":** Rich, *Of Woman Born*, 194.

159 **"affirming fatalism":** Two quotes from Rich, *Of Woman Born*, 28–29.

160   **"beauty, humor":** Three quotes from Rich, *Of Woman Born*, 194.

161   **"hand-to-mouth":** Two quotes from Rich, *Of Woman Born*, 194.

161   **"the institution of motherhood":** Rich, *Of Woman Born*, 195.

161   **In a letter:** See Holladay, *The Power of Adrienne Rich*, 213.

162   **"What does not change":** Adrienne Rich, epigraph to *The Will to Change* in *Collected Poems*, 298.

162   **"ribs of the disaster":** Three quotes from Adrienne Rich, "Diving into the Wreck," in *Collected Poems*, 372.

162   **"leap":** Two quotes from Adrienne Rich, "From a Survivor," in *Collected Poems*, 397.

163   **"massacred":** Rich, *Of Woman Born*, 13.

163   **"deep, fatalistic pessimism":** Rich, *On Lies, Secrets, and Silence*, 49.

163   **"the very plenitude":** Two quotes from Rich, *Of Woman Born*, xxxii.

164   **"a ground hedged":** Rich, *Of Woman Born*, 15.

164   **"fulfilling even in its sorrows":** Rich, *Of Woman Born*, 15.

165   **but marital rape:** See footnote in Rich, *Of Woman Born*, 74.

165   **"this crossroads of":** Rich, *Of Woman Born*, 61–62.

166   **"whiny":** See Gail Collins's introduction to Betty Friedan, *The Feminine Mystique* (New York: W. W. Norton, 1963; 2013 reissue), xiv. Collins celebrates the book but lends a sympathetic ear to this critique.

168   **"The daily fight":** Hannah Arendt, *The Human Condition* (Chicago: University of Chicago Press, 1958), 101.

168   **"The million tiny stitches":** Rich, *On Lies, Secrets, and Silence*, 205.

169   **"activity of world-protection":** Rich, *On Lies, Secrets, and Silence*, 205.

169   **"source of her awe":** Rich, *Of Woman Born*, 126–27.

170   **"truly create new life":** Rich, *Of Woman Born*, 285–86.

170   **"forgotten future":** Adrienne Rich, "Poetry and the Forgotten Future,"

in Rich, *A Human Eye: Essays on Art in Society, 1997–2008* (New York: W. W. Norton, 2009), 143.

171 **"wild patience"**: See Adrienne Rich, *A Wild Patience Has Taken Me This Far: Poems 1978–1981* (New York: W. W. Norton, 1981).

CHAPTER 7: ANCIENT PROPERTIES

173 **"Do you have any future plans"**: Judith Wilson, "A Conversation with Toni Morrison," in *Conversations with Toni Morrison*, ed. Danille Taylor-Guthrie (Jackson: University Press of Mississippi, 1994), 136.

174 **"ability to hold"**: Wilson, "A Conversation with Toni Morrison," 131.

174 **"ancient properties"**: Charles Ruas, "Toni Morrison," in Taylor-Guthrie, *Conversations with Toni Morrison*, 104.

174 **"a ship"**: Taylor-Guthrie, *Conversations with Toni Morrison*, 102.

174 **America's female workforce:** See Esteban Ortiz-Ospina and Sandra Tzvetkova, "Working Women: Key Facts and Trends in Female Labor Force Participation," Our World in Data, October 16, 2017, https://ourworldindata .org/female-labor-force-participation-key-facts.

174 **"If you kill the ancestors"**: Two quotes from Wilson, "A Conversation with Toni Morrison," 131.

175 **"What you do to children"**: Toni Morrison, *God Help the Child* (New York: Vintage, 2015), 43.

175 **"That's my house"**: Four quotes from "Toni Morrison Remembers," BBC, Summer 2015, https://www.youtube.com/watch?v=-OURXCUdeOA.

176 **"grew up in a"**: Morrison, "A Slow Walk of Trees," in *What Moves at the Margin: Selected Nonfiction*, ed. Carolyn C. Denard (Jackson: University Press of Mississippi, 2008), 7.

176 **"unreconstructed black pessimist"**: Three quotes from Morrison, "A Slow Walk of Trees," 8.

177 **"irrevocable and permanent"**: Morrison, "A Slow Walk of Trees," 5.

177 **"racial vertigo"**: Morrison, "A Slow Walk of Trees," 8.

178 **"the type who tore"**: Emma Brockes, "Toni Morrison: 'I Want to Feel What I Feel. Even If It's Not Happiness,'" *Guardian*, April 13, 2012.

178 **"nest and the adventure"**: Claudia Tate, "Toni Morrison," in *Conversations with Toni Morrison*, 161.

179 **"perfectly content with"**: Cited in Nadra Nittle, *Toni Morrison's Spiritual Vision: Faith, Folktales, and Feminism in Her Life and Literature* (Minneapolis: Fortress Press, 2021), 73.

179 **"have held, have been given"**: Robert Stepto, "Intimate Things in Place: A Conversation with Toni Morrison," in Taylor-Guthrie, *Conversations with Toni Morrison*, 17.

179 **"Black people believe"**: Mel Watkins, "Talk with Toni Morrison," in Taylor-Guthrie, *Conversations with Toni Morrison*, 46.

179 **"the strange stuff"**: Stephanie Paulsell, "Reading Toni Morrison in Advent," *Christian Century*, December 2, 2019. Cited in Nittle, *Toni Morrison's Spiritual Vision*, 76.

180 **Morrison chose a new name**: See Nittle, *Toni Morrison's Spiritual Vision*, 54, 56–57.

181 **"one of the most beautiful"**: Adam Langer, "Star Power," in *Toni Morrison: Conversations*, ed. Carolyn C. Denard (Jackson: University Press of Mississippi, 2008), 211. Cited in Stephanie Li, *Toni Morrison: A Biography* (Santa Barbara, CA: Greenwood Press, 2010), 12.

181 **"what moves at the margin"**: Toni Morrison, "The Nobel Lecture in Literature," in Morrison, *What Moves at the Margin*, 206.

181 **"it is nothing less"**: Toni Morrison, "A Knowing So Deep," in Morrison, *What Moves at the Margin*, 31.

183 **"psychological murder"**: Toni Morrison, *The Bluest Eye* (New York: Vintage, 1970), x.

184 **"The real liberation"**: Two quotes from Brockes, "Toni Morrison: 'I Want to Feel What I Feel.'"

185 **"wholly free"**: Stepto, "Intimate Things in Place," 23.

186 **"I will not let"**: Gloria Naylor, "A Conversation: Gloria Naylor and Toni Morrison," in Taylor-Guthrie, *Conversations with Toni Morrison*, 207.

187 **"'I watched her'"**: Two quotes from Naylor, "A Conversation," 207.

187 **"terrible"**: Toni Morrison, "The Source of Self-Regard,"in Toni Morrison, *The Source of Self-Regard: Selected Essays, Speeches, and Meditations* (New York: Alfred A. Knopf, 2019), 309.

188 **"is like the world"**: Toni Morrison, *Beloved* (New York: Penguin, 1987), 33.

188 **"the details of her birth"**: Two quotes from Morrison, *Beloved*, 29.

188 **"rip was a breakup"**: Morrison, *Beloved*, 84.

189 **"seeds in which"**: Morrison, *Beloved*, 84.

189 **"Let the children come!"**: Morrison, *Beloved*, 87.

189 **"your life-holding womb"**: Morrison, *Beloved*, 89.

190 **"A woman loved something"**: Two quotes from Naylor, "A Conversation," 207.

190 **"had arrived at"**: Morrison, *Beloved*, 250.

190 **"secret by which"**: Herbert Gutman, *The Black Family in Slavery and Freedom, 1750–1925* (New York: Pantheon, 1976), 80–81, note. Cited in Angela Y. Davis, *Women, Race and Class* (New York: Random House, 1982), 204.

191 **"property that reproduced"**: Morrison, *Beloved*, 228.

191 **"Black women"**: Two quotes from Davis, *Women, Race and Class*, 204.

192 **This was true**: Donna L. Hoyert, "Maternal Mortality Rates in the United States, 2020," NCHS Health E-Stats, 2022, https://dx.doi.org/10.15620/cdc:113967.

192 **"During the early stages"**: bell hooks, *Feminist Theory: From Margin to Center* (New York: Routledge, 1984), 133.

192 **She wrote about how**: bell hooks, *Feminism Is for Everybody: Passionate Politics* (Cambridge, MA: South End Press, 2000), 6.

193 **"committed to survival"**: All Walker quotes from Alice Walker, *In Search of Our Mothers' Gardens* (New York: Harcourt, 1983), xi–xii.

193 **"black, lesbian"**: https://www.poetryfoundation.org/poets/audre-lorde.

193 **"we must never close our eyes"**: Audre Lorde, *Sister Outsider: Essays and Speeches* (Berkeley, CA: Crossing Press, 1984), 101.

194 **"come coil with me"**: Lucille Clifton, "brothers," in *The Collected Poems of Lucille Clifton 1965–2010*, ed. Kevin Young and Michael S. Glaser (Rochester, NY: BOA Editions, 2012), 466.

194 **"this creation is so fierce"**: Lucille Clifton, "adam thinking," in Young and Glaser, *Collected Poems*, 399.

194 **"Nature wants it done"**: Bonnie Angelo, "The Pain of Being Black: An Interview with Toni Morrison," in Taylor-Guthrie, *Conversations with Toni Morrison*, 260.

195 **"Your baby is beautiful"**: Angelo, "The Pain of Being Black," 260.

195 **"biological life process"**: Two quotes from Hannah Arendt, *The Human Condition*, 2nd ed. (Chicago: University of Chicago Press, 1958), 37.

195 **"illegal, anarchic"**: Three quotes from Morrison, *The Source of Self-Regard*, 282.

196 **"something to be first recognized"**: All *Sula* quotes from Toni Morrison, *Sula* (New York: Vintage, 1973), 118.

196 **"We believe that evil has a natural place"**: Two quotes from Jean Parker, "Complexity: Toni Morrison's Women," in Taylor-Guthrie, *Conversations with Toni Morrison*, 62.

196 **"beautiful, magical best thing"**: Morrison, *Beloved*, 261.

197 **"belly big and tight"**: Morrison, *Beloved*, 261.

197 **"on the biological span"**: Two quotes from Morrison, "The Future of Time: Literature and Diminished Expectations," in Morrison, *What Moves at the Margin*, 172.

197 **"is about to take"**: Morrison, "The Future of Time," 186.

197 **"the best of all"**: Friedrich Nietzsche, *The Birth of Tragedy: Out of the Spirit of Music*, trans. Shaun Whiteside and ed. Michael Tanner (New York: Penguin, 1993), 22.

198 **"I didn't ask"**: Two quotes from Bill Moyers, "A Conversation with Toni Morrison," in Taylor-Guthrie, *Conversations with Toni Morrison*, 267–68.

198 **"our conscience"**: Oprah Winfrey (@oprah), "In the beginning was the Word," Instagram, August 6, 2019, https://www.instagram.com/p/B01OMclhby2/.

198 **"Suffer little children"**: Luke 18:16 (King James Bible).

199 **"I hate to say it"**: Morrison, *God Help the Child*, 4.

199 **"Now she's pregnant"**: Morrison, *God Help the Child*, 178.

199 **"You . . . are the touchstone"**: Morrison, "A Knowing So Deep," 33.

Epilogue

203 **Global mortality rates rose**: "Death Rate, Crude (per 1,000 People)," World Bank, https://data.worldbank.org/indicator/SP.DYN.CDRT.IN?end=2020&start=1960&view=chart, accessed July 2, 2022.

203 **fertility rates dropped**: "Fertility Rate, Total (Births per Woman)," World Bank, https://data.worldbank.org/indicator/SP.DYN.TFRT.IN?end=2020&start=1960&view=chart, accessed July 2, 2022.

203 **"Even in the darkest of times"**: Hannah Arendt, *Men in Dark Times* (New York: Harcourt, Brace, 1970), ix.

203 **"were we led"**: T. S. Eliot, "Journey of the Magi," in *Collected Poems: 1909–1962* (London: Faber and Faber, 1974).

204 **The world**: All quotes from Hannah Arendt, *The Promise of Politics*, ed. Jerome Kohn (New York: Schocken, 2005), 201–4.

206 **"shocked wonder"**: Hannah Arendt, *The Human Condition*, 2nd ed. (Chicago: University of Chicago Press, 1958), 302.

206 **"disappeared from the world"**: Hannah Arendt, *The Life of the Mind:*

The Groundbreaking Investigation of How We Think (New York: Harcourt, 1971), 83.

206   **"thinking without a banister":** Hannah Arendt, *Thinking Without a Banister: Essays in Understanding, 1953–1975*, ed. Jerome Kohn (New York: Schocken, 2018).

206   **"These questions":** Arendt, *The Promise of Politics*, 204.

207   **"mark of resistance":** Two quotes from Adrienne Rich, "A Mark of Resistance," *Poetry*, August 1957.

Index